BLACKJACK
SECRETS

BLACKJACK
SECRETS

A Handbook for Beginners

SKYHORSE PUBLISHING

Skyhorse Publishing books may be purchased in bulk at special
discounts for sales promotion, corporate gifts, fund-raising, or
educational purposes. Special editions can also be created to
specifications. For details, contact the Special Sales Department,
Skyhorse Publishing, 307 West 36th Street, 11th Floor, New York, NY
10018 or info@skyhorsepublishing.com.

Skyhorse® and Skyhorse Publishing® are registered trademarks of
Skyhorse Publishing, Inc.®, a Delaware corporation.

www.skyhorsepublishing.com

10 9 8 7 6 5 4 3 2 1

Library of Congress Cataloging-in-Publication Data is available on file.
ISBN: 978-1-61608-314-4

Printed in China

Contents

PLAYING AT THE TABLE

ODDS & ENDS

Blackjack Secrets
could not have been accomplished
without the support of my family.

I would like to say a special thanks to
David and Curtis.

Introduction

Welcome to *Blackjack Secrets*.

I started writing my previous book, *The Most Powerful Blackjack Manual*, at the end of the nineties. Since I finished writing that book, I continue to play regularly, but contrary to many experts, I have not turned into a professional and moved to Vegas. Of course, I play there along with Atlantic City, not to mention Monte Carlo and many other places. As I mentioned in my first book, I have remained a part-time player and still have fun playing blackjack. As I used to joke at the table, as soon as we make some money, we'll have a lot of fun (have you ever had fun when you lost?). You might ask yourself, sure, why not? Despite the fact that I continue to love the game, it is not in my nature to play for hours every day as this would make life too monotonous.

The results of my more than thirty years of experience will be summarized in this book, complete with the last five to six years since I wrote my last book.

I continue to work as an architect, but I retired as a teacher long ago. Although, I kept my desire to teach, and this is one of the reasons why I have decided to write my second book. While writing, I still feel like I am a professor giving a lecture.

Just like I said at the end of my first book, I still don't want to include my picture for the simple fact that I still want to play and not to be recognized.

Another reason why I decided to write this book was because I feel that after three decades of experience, I can provide valuable secrets not only for beginners but for intermediate players as well—and the only reason I am hesitant to use the word *expert* is because, after all these years, I am still doubtful as to who I can consider to be an *expert player.*

As we know, a higher bettor doesn't mean a better player. For a long time I thought that those who played with a $50–$100 (or higher) initial bet must be skilled. I know today that this is not necessarily true, and I also wholeheartedly recommend my book to those $100 beginner-expert players who may not even realize that they are, on average, putting $5,000–$7,000 in action per hour.

In my first book, I wrote in detail about the requirement of the *externals* of the game (knowledge of the game) and the *internals* of the game (your emotions, and emotional and financial expectations). To learn the *externals* (basic strategy, money management, etc.) is relatively easy and takes no more than a few days or weeks. But mastering the *internals* of the game takes much longer and is much, *much* harder. Someone who is unable to master the *internals* or underestimates the

meaning will never be a constant winner and will never be able to take home a piece of the cake.

In this book, I summarize and explain those crucial secrets that have a <u>deciding importance in everyday play</u>. Even if you do not know anything else about the game, just follow these secrets and you will improve your skill significantly.

If you need just any kind of secrets, surf the Internet. You will find a lot of useless . . .

If you need *real* secrets, then this book is for you!

At the time of writing this book, I assume that you, the reader, have some knowledge and an understanding of the basic rules of the game, how to play the game (basic strategy), when to quit, how to manage your money, how to control your game, and so on. Due to this fact, I will not go into details about the basics. If you are not familiar with these basics, I suggest that you read my first book.

Before I offer my blackjack secrets, I would like to mention that it is not a bad idea to know the origin of the *name of the game* that we play.

The origin of blackjack is somewhat unclear. Most believe blackjack entered the gaming industry in French casinos during the 1700s. It has been played in North America since the 1800s. In the early eighteenth century, French casinos had played a game called "Vingt-et-un," which means "Twenty-one" (20 and 1). When a player had been dealt a jack and ace of spades as their first two cards, they had won the hand and were paid out extra. Jack being a vital card, and the ace of spades being a black card, the combination of the two coined the name "Black-Jack."

Let's get started.

THEORY
(To Learn at Home)

You Have to Know the
OBJECT OF THE GAME

(The object of the game is to beat the dealer.)

It is obvious that when we sit down to play, we have to know what we are playing for—what is the *object of the game*. When it comes time to determine the object of the game, even the greatest authors make mistakes and do not tell both sides of the truth.

When we discuss the object of the game, we talk about the object from the player's standpoint. The dealer has no object to the game because the dealer must follow the rules of the casino.

I firmly believe that the name of the game is to win money. We can also say, however, that the object is to make money. I like to use the phrase "make" a little bit more than "win," even though the gist is the same. Anybody can win; he just needs a little luck. Very few of us can make money because it requires knowledge, skill, and first of all, self-control. In order to make money, we have to beat the dealer. For this reason:

The objective of the casino game of blackjack is simply to beat the dealer.

You can achieve this in two different ways:
1. Having your cards total higher than the dealer's without your total exceeding 21 (if the value of your cards exceeds 21, you automatically lose).
2. To have any "valid hand" while the dealer busts.

This second way is just as important as the first. These two possibilities present the whole picture.

Many people (and sometimes even authors) forget the second possibility. Actually, some players think the object is to get as close to 21 as possible or (which is even worse— almost stupid) to draw cards that total 21. You should forget it forever.

You can even read this type of misinformation in many casinos' gaming guides.

When I want to get a picture of how reliable a certain book or Internet website is, for me it's always a good idea to check how they determine the object of the game.

If they say, "The basic objective of the game is that you want to have a hand value that is closer to 21 than that of the dealer without going over 21," I know they aren't telling the full "story." Or something that means the same, "Score a higher hand than the dealer without busting."

However, if they say, "The object of the game is to get as close to 21 as possible," I know right away that this book or website is not for me.

How can you trust anybody who doesn't even know (or even worse, someone who doesn't want to tell you) the object of the game?

You Should Know Why to
STAND-HIT-DOUBLE-SPLIT

(When we double or split, most of the time we will not get a good card.)

When the original two cards have been dealt to all players and the dealer doesn't have a blackjack, the game goes on. We now all have the original hands of two cards. The dealer continues to deal the cards clockwise, starting back at the beginning with the first baseman. From then on, it's <u>your</u> decision what to do.

I would like to reiterate that your decisions *cannot* depend on your feelings. Playing by your feelings is a foolish way of gambling.

All of our decisions depend on the dealer's upcard and on our original hand.

Our decisions have to be based on these facts and not on feelings. Any book's (or website's) basic strategy chart tells you what decision you have to make based on the cards that you have, depending on the dealer's upcard.

The basic strategy is nothing more than a set of rules that help determine *when* and *what* decision to make in order to minimize the casino's advantage. It tells the player when to stand or draw, when to double down, and when to split pairs. It tells us the playing decisions that we have to make to improve our chances of winning. The basic strategy

does not usually turn a losing hand into a winning hand. It only allows you to lose less. During the game you have to decide when to stand? hit? double? split? take insurance? These decisions cannot be based on our feelings. Making a decision is not easy. It takes skill, study, discipline, and patience. These attributes are very important since if we know what decisions we have to keep to, then doing so seems easy.

If you learned the rules, then basically you don't have to make a decision—you just have to <u>employ</u> the <u>correct decision at the right place</u>. To learn the rules (basic strategy) is the easier part of the "homework." The hardest part is discipline—are you able to maintain self-control and follow the rules all the time?

I have to tell you that since the basic strategy was first publicized, there have been disagreements about how much *flexibility* we should allow in these rules (which is determined by us) and how much we should keep to the original strategy. Even if you study and compare famous authors' charts, you will realize that while the majority of the chart is similar, they are not 100% identical. Some players are more aggressive and others are more conservative. One thing is for sure: the basic strategy works only in the long term. Anything can happen in a given night. As I sometimes joke at the table-side, if you are lucky enough to be alive for 200 years, the chart will work for you.

The player has four basic options when it comes time to make a decision: stand, hit, double down, or split. I will show you <u>why</u> you make these decisions.

Generally speaking, we have two possibilities:

A. If the dealer has a standing card (7 or higher), hit until hard 17.

B. If the dealer has a potential bust card (6 or lower), let him bust.

1. STAND

It is a player's decision not to draw any additional cards.

If we know we've got a hand with the best chance to beat the dealer, we do not ask for additional cards.

<u>Why do we stand?</u> There are two reasons:

1. If the hand is strong enough to win (19, 20, 21) or high enough (hard 17, 18) to have a good chance of going over 21.

2. If the dealer has a strong chance to go over 21. In this situation, we give the dealer the chance to go over. For instance, if the player's hand is 10, 2, and the dealer's upcard is a 6, we stand. Let the dealer bust first.

Why do we <u>not</u> stand? *Never ever stand just because you feel the next card has to be a big one* and you will go over! For instance, the dealer's upcard is a 9 and the player's original hand is a 10, 5 (= hard 15). If we could feel (figure out) the next card, the casinos would not be in business. But they are!

2. HIT

To request one or more additional cards from the dealer.

To hit a hand and go over 21 is called *busting*. It is also known as *breaking*. When <u>we</u> bust, we have lost and are out of the game for that round. But note! If the <u>dealer</u> busts, they lose only to those players who still have a valid hand. What a difference! For this reason, if the dealer <u>and</u> the player both bust, the player still loses. This is the biggest edge the casino has over us. We cannot do anything to combat this. It is just a part of the rules of the game.

Here is a question that you might ask: "Why would we risk a hit if we can bust and lose immediately?" We don't hit all the time when we can bust. But, if the dealer probably will have a 17 or higher total, there is no reason to stand on a stiff total. We have a good chance to lose our bet without even trying to improve our hand.

<u>Why do we hit?</u> We are asking for more cards in order to improve our total. A player may draw as many cards as he wants, as long as the total does not exceed 21.

3. DOUBLE DOWN

This option allows the player to double the size of his bet (you may make a second wager no higher than the amount of your original bet) and receive only one more card. Double down is one of the advantages the player has against the casino. Go for it!

I do not know how many times I've heard players say, "I never double."

Leave those losers in their ruts.

Any restriction by the casino on doubling increases the house's advantage.

When one of the two original cards is an ace, it's referred to as soft doubling because the player has a soft hand initially.

<u>Why are we doubling?</u>

We try to make twice as much money when the dealer is weak!

Remember that <u>we are not doubling to get a good card</u>. The odds are against us getting a good card most of the time. Here is just one example: We have 11 and double down. What can we get? If we get an ace or 2, 3, 4, 5, 6, or 7, we will not have a "winning hand" (I'm not saying we cannot win—but the theoretical winning hand is 19 or higher). This is 7 out of 13 possible cards or 53.8%. And remember, we had 11—quite possibly the best doubling down hand. I'm not saying that I'm a happy camper when I get a 5 doubling on 11, but it is not the end of the world. After all, most of the time we are doubling because we hope the dealer will bust.

You can also <u>double for less</u> than the initial wager; however, it is not a great idea. We are doubling to make more money; therefore it doesn't make sense to double for less. Either *double* or don't double at all.

4. SPLITTING PAIRS

This option allows the player to separate the first two cards dealt if they are a pair creating two separate hands.

Just because we have the possibility to split it doesn't mean we <u>have</u> to split. Some players think that if they have been dealt a pair (a potential split hand), they should (or have to) split. No. Never split a pair <u>just</u> because you were dealt them! When someone receives a queen and a king and asks if they can split, they not only reveal that they are a very weak player but also that they don't even know the rules. In other words, it is almost like saying out loud, "I'm such a bad player that I have failed to learn even the basic rules of the game."

A special rule applies to the splitting of aces. When a pair of aces are split, you normally receive only one card on each hand. It's not allowed to split again if you get another ace. In addition, if the player receives a 10-value card on one or both of the split aces, the hand counts as 21 and not as a blackjack (remember the definition of blackjack: If the *original* hand consists of an ace and a 10-value card, then it's a blackjack).

Why are we splitting pairs?

There are two reasons.

The first is exactly the same as what I said at doubling: we try to make twice (or even four times) as much money when the dealer is weak.

The second is we try to improve our hand. If you receive a like card on a split, don't even waste a second thinking about it. Just split them again!

Let me give you one more piece of advice:

<u>Never let yourself be influenced by the size of your bet</u> if it comes time to double down or split pairs. Do not hesitate. Just do it. Make as much money as possible! This is one of our biggest advantages against the casino. If you're afraid to put out another $100 chip (the number can be anything), then you cannot afford the $100 bet.

Don't Make the BIGGEST MISTAKE

(Not asking for a card on 16 against the dealer's face card is a proposition for losing.)

Until we reach a certain level, we always make mistakes when we play at the table. It cannot be in doubt that the decisions have to be made according to the basic strategy chart.

As soon as we deviate from what's there, we've already made a mistake.

The severity of the mistake, however, can affect us in different ways. For instance, if we don't double down on a ten against the dealer's five, it is of course a mistake, but the "only" consequence will be half of the expected win.

I will demonstrate an example that will always affect us negatively. Not only in a sense that we will win less, but that we will actually lose.

When the dealer is in a standing position (upcard: 7, 8, 9, 10, J, Q, K, ace), there is no reason to stand on a stiff total—we try to "catch" him by hitting. But the same old question comes up once again, "Why would we risk a hit if we can bust and lose immediately?" Because we have a good chance of losing our bet without even trying to improve our hand.

Here is one example. The dealer's upcard is a 10. Our two cards are a 9 and a 7 (total of 16). I know, it is a typical losing hand. When I get this hand, I feel like a baseball team when they need a grand slam but nobody is on base.

What is the correct play? All of us have seen that a great number of players stand at 16. In fact, even at 15 in this case because they are thinking about the possibility of breaking. *I can tell you that standing on 16 or less against the dealer's 10 is the <u>biggest mistake</u> anybody can make at the blackjack table!*

Why? Let's look at the possibilities of what kind of card the dealer can turn over on his 10. If the dealer gets a 7, 8, 9, 10, J, Q, K, A, then his hand will be 17 or higher and we lose (with the ace, he has a blackjack).

This is 8 cards out of a possible 13. If I don't even observe the other five, I have already lost the fight since we are losers 8 out of 13 cases (which is 61.54%). Then, I'm not even taking into consideration what happens if the dealer gets a 2, 3, 4, 5, or 6. With the drawing of an additional card, the chances that the dealer will beat me are almost 50% yet again.

This is why it is the biggest mistake in blackjack to stand below 17 if the dealer's upcard is a 7 or higher. Please do not stand! Take your chance to improve your hand, and try to make it stronger! If you lose, you lose. At least you can say, "I have tried and did not give up without even attempting to get a better hand."

After showing you the biggest mistake, let me show you the <u>most foolish play</u>. We have two 10-value cards. One of the most beautiful hands in the game! Do you know that this hand makes the most money for us after a blackjack? So why should we do anything else other than stand? Don't even think about splitting them. Be happy to have them!—and stand all the time regardless of what kind of card the dealer has. I don't care if anybody comes up with any kind of theory regarding why it's good to split tens or faces. I'll be short. Of all the foolish plays, splitting 10s is probably the most stupid. Never ever split them up!

When you see a player standing with a(ny) soft 17, you'll know that he is a loser. Now I can tell you that if somebody splits 10s, they are not just a loser but they are telling you, "I don't know what I am doing here." They are throwing away a winning hand. Don't be greedy and (don't) try to turn a winning hand into two winning hands. Most of the time it just doesn't work!

Remember What the WINNING HAND Is

(If you have 18, you have next to nothing.)

If I offered you a blackjack table where the casino would guarantee you a constant hand of 18, would you go for it? Yes? I can tell you that the majority of the players would say yes without even thinking about it for a second. Before you answer, let me ask you one more thing: Do you know what the average winning hand in blackjack is?

Before you answer this question, take a look at the next table. I won't load you down with a lot of tables, and even the ones I put in won't be too difficult. You don't have to be a rocket scientist to understand them. Please don't get scared and turn the page, saying, "Thank you for coming out, but tables are not for me." Leave this to the losers. The 95%. They don't even want to belong to the 5%. There is no rule that says you have to remember all of these numbers.

The numbers could vary only slightly depending on the number of decks and rule variations.

Dealer Final-Hand Probabilities

Dealer final-hand value	%	Cumulative % total
Blackjack	4.83	4.83
21	7.36	12.19
20	17.58	29.77
19	13.48	43.25
18	13.81	**57.06**
17	14.58	71.64
Bust	28.36	100.00

What do these figures show? What we are mostly interested in is one number. The **bolded** 57.06.

The dealer, in 57.06% of the cases, will have an 18 or higher card. Thus, if we have 18, we cannot beat the dealer. If in 57.06% of the cases we cannot beat the dealer, then we can only beat him in 42.94% (100–57.06) of the cases. Which is a lot less than 50%! This is why you should not go for a constant hand of 18. Eighteen is just not enough on the average to win if the dealer does not bust.

Or it can be put this way: If you have 18:
The dealer will beat you with a 19 or higher—43.25% of the time.
The dealer will lose to you with a 17 or bust—42.94% of the time

(14.58+28.36).

(13.81% of the hands will be a tie of course, when both of you have 18).

Consequently, you will be losing 0.31% (43.25–42.94) of the hands with a constant 18 in the long term.

This means that **the average winning hand in blackjack is** over 18, which is **19-20-21 or blackjack**.

Let's also remember one more thing: *The dealer will bust less than 30% (28.36) of the time.*

After this demonstration, I would think it's easy to answer the question, "Would you go for a constant hand of 18?" No, you shouldn't. It is just not enough to win in the long term.

Even most dealers don't know what the winning hand in blackjack is, otherwise they would not say (showing a face card when somebody gets 18), "This is good." This is just not good enough.

We already know the average winning hand is over 18. Therefore, if we have 17 or 18, it's just not enough. However, we cannot hit on a 17 or an 18 since only the minority of the available cards will not bust our hand. What can we do? Nothing but expect to lose. If you still don't lose, be happy! Knowing the basic strategy cannot make a losing hand a winning hand, but we can *minimize* our losses.

Learn What You Can EXPECT
from the Game

(If you expect a quick big win, don't play blackjack.)

There is no denying the necessity of the knowledge, but the basic knowledge itself is not enough. There are a lot of good players with good knowledge, and they still are not able to make money. Those people expect more from this game than it has to offer. They think they have more chances than they actually have, and they think they can win more money than the game has to offer. They expect more.

Here is an example. Remember, when players are complaining at the table, "An ace [or 10 or face] again?" when they see two or three in a row, that means that they did not expect it. In one deck there are sixteen 10-value cards + four aces = 20 cards. This accounts for 38.46% of the total cards (52). In other words, the dealer will show up an ace or a 10-value card on average almost 2 out of 5 times. Don't be surprised! You have to expect and accept that this is how it will happen. When you hear somebody "complain," you *know* they *don't know* what to expect. They say nothing more than, "We are the weak players."

We have to know what to expect. Otherwise, we won't be able to handle the game emotionally. If we are not capable emotionally of what is happening to us, then we are losers. Just like a roller coaster. Once up, once down. Big climbs. Big drops. Furthermore, blackjack is a very tough game. Blackjack is an emotional game. It is very hard to beat.

You have to know that **the deal is not between you and the casino, but between you and yourself.** We have to see clearly that the casino's advantages (we take the first card, casino has an unlimited bankroll, the rules set by the casinos, etc.) are facts. We cannot do anything against those factors, we cannot change them, but we have to know them to be able to accommodate and deal with them. And since we cannot influence these factors, we have to work on the things that give us the advantages and that depend on our behavior and knowledge. We have to know everything about these factors. We have to make an effort to be perfect. It is not enough to know just *some things*. We have to know *everything*.

With everything taken into consideration, the house will have a 0.5–1.0% advantage over us. We can't expect for the casino not to have an advantage over us, since they would not have been in business for very long if the odds were even.

We should never forget and you have to know, accept, and expect that **we are the underdogs**.

If it were true that a basic knowledge of the game is enough to win, then all the good players would be winners. The facts, however, don't really indicate this. In other words, to know the basics of the game only constitutes having the knowledge necessary to play, but not adequate knowledge to be a winner. The basic knowledge of the game by itself isn't enough, since there are many good players who, on a regular basis, only play even with the casino.

I firmly believe that one of the foremost reasons why people leave the Blackjack battlefield as a loser is because <u>they expect much more</u> than is possible, <u>than they can</u> realistically <u>expect</u>

from this game! We would like to believe that we have more of a chance, but we have to know that we don't. Please do not confuse what <u>we would like</u> with what we <u>know</u>.

In contradiction to others who have written on this topic, first I do not blame these players' lack of knowledge <u>only</u>—although in a lot of cases this is a significant factor too—since this in itself is not the main reason to lose, but the lack of knowing what they can expect. Blackjack is not a game where you can win big money fast, or indeed win on a constant basis. You have to build your success step by step, over and over again. Most authors blame the lack of knowledge for losing. We cannot doubt the significance of this knowledge, but to blame this factor entirely is not nearly enough. What is expected and what actually happens are of course two different things.

By the short term, I mean playing once or occasionally; as people say, anything can happen. I can't say it enough times, "<u>In the short term, everything is expected!</u>" In short, things that have to happen will happen. In playing the game, speaking in the long term, things will happen that I know and that I expect.

Never in my life have I sat down to play when I set up a $200 goal (and this number can be any favorable number) that I have to achieve. This is even more the case because I know that unavoidably there will be losing days. Do you see any sense in setting up a $200 goal when you know that you can conceivably lose, which is just part of the game? There are, of course, goals that guide me in my game, but these are totally different than saying I will win *x* dollars on any given day.

For example, I don't think that anybody has to be a rocket scientist to see that if you play with a bigger initial bet, then you can expect bigger winnings. However, this means that you also have to face a possible bigger loss. And since no one can promise us that all of our playing will be profitable, given that there will be losing days, this is again a fact that we have to accept and something we have to prepare for.

The "art" of making money in the casino is not a simple and onetime "exercise." We have to prove everything bit by bit, over and over again. Just get it into your head this way: There is nothing wrong with making a "small" amount of money. If you want to make more, you surely have to increase your initial unit bet.

Just think about this. How many times have you gone home from the casino as a loser after playing for 5 hours? If in those 5 hours you would have made only 10 units, imagine what a big difference that would have been! After 5 hours of playing, 10 units won, and for comparison, let's "just" lose the same amount. That's already a 20-unit difference in just one day. Even at the $10 table, that is a $200 difference. How many of us can afford to lose this on a daily basis? We all know how to calculate what would happen if our unit bet were to be $100.

Dreams? Yes, you can dream. But dreamers are losers.

You have to know what to expect . . . there is no way to win more hands than the dealer. The average winning hand in blackjack is over 18, which is 19-20-21 or blackjack. On average, we will get blackjack on every 20th hand, the dealer will bust in 28.36% of the total cases, the dealer will show an ace or a 10-value card almost 40% of the time and the list goes on. You can find all of these figures in my first book, *The Most Powerful Blackjack Manual.*

From the moment that you put your expectations into place, your whole relationship to the game will change irreversibly. From that moment, you will never ever enter the casino with the idea that "My plan for today is to win *x* amount, or big money."

As I said, blackjack is an emotional game. Just like a roller coaster. Once up, once down. Big climbs. Big drops. In closing, I would like to explain how big these ups and downs can be. On average, the game fluctuates 10–20 units.

This of course doesn't mean that you will win or lose this many hands in a row. This means that the bankroll that you have at the table will grow or shrink by this amount. Doesn't this seem like a lot? Many don't even believe it. How else could you explain someone at the $50 table who is up, say, $700–$800 and is not happy? They expect more than what the game has to offer. There simply isn't anything more for the game to offer.

Believe me, 10–20 units is quite a lot. Don't expect more. In most cases, don't even expect this much. Clearly, we never know when a winning streak will end. Because of this, we will almost always lose the last few hands of a session. (The only exception might be when after a big comeback we suddenly quit.) If you are above the expected 10–20 units, be very cautious and unconditionally quit right away if you start heading south.

Blackjack is an emotional game.

If the dealer busts on a bust card, we accept it since we expected it. If the dealer makes 21 on his bust card, we are frustrated. In other words, if what we expect happens, then our joy will not be as broad as our sorrow when the opposite of the expected happens.

Keep your emotions low key. You cannot be happy *or* unhappy after each and every hand. Leave it to the Saturday evening players. They want to be emotionally involved. They want to have action. They want to have a "good" time. They just don't know what to expect.

Don't stress yourself out at the blackjack table.

If you know what to expect, you will dream less but you will part from the casino disappointed on a less frequent basis.

You Have to Have Adequate BANKROLL

(You have to decide your minimum bet according to your bankroll—your bankroll is not decided by the minimum bet.)

You have to have the power.

If you don't have adequate bankroll, it will make you tense and you will not be able to survive the ups and downs.

You cannot be worried that you do not have enough bankroll.

To play blackjack and make money is not the type of business where you can go into the casino with a relatively trifling sum, and then come out with a significant amount of money. You can hit the jackpot with a slot machine, but we are talking about playing blackjack.

Most of the books suggest a high bankroll. The numbers are based on different—simpler or more complicated—card-counting methods. I don't want to enter into details, since I don't deal with card counting. One thing is for sure—how I play in the casino does not necessitate a high-starting bankroll. However, it is true that the available amount of money (your bankroll) will determine what you can count on making.

Just like in any other business (and I consider making money playing blackjack a business), <u>you cannot make money without money</u>. I think this is a type of truth that is known by everybody. For some

reason, when people sit down to play blackjack, they forget it and start to chase dreams. If your money allows you to play at the $10 table only, you can expect $20–$30 profit per 100 hands. If you don't accept it, you'll be an inevitable loser.

Many times I had the feeling that some authors of books consider the reader a kid. How else can I explain when they suggest to not spend more than 2% of your annual income for gambling, or to never take more than one-tenth of your total bankroll into the casino, or to divide your starting capital into three sessions, and so on. Come on. Give me a break. Forget it.

How many times did you hear or read this: Do not risk more money than you can afford to lose? Sure it is true, but there is not much we can do with this type of generality.

You are the only one who knows your own situation. You are the one taking care of your own money. Nobody will write a check for you to recover your losses. It is your money, and you have to know what to do.

I can state with certainty, the majority of gamblers have absolutely no idea what a bankroll is and why they have to (or should) manage their money. They usually go to the casino, take whatever spare money they have, and hope they can win something. After losing that money, the next time they continue exactly the same way. They form the group who go to the casino with $300–$500 and believe they have to pay that much money for this type of entertainment. They think they will have a good time for their money, and the losses were the price for the entertainment. Here is how I think: we can have a good time <u>and</u> we do not have to lose.

In order to be able to create a bankroll, let me define what the bankroll is.

A bankroll is cold, hard cash that you have for the purpose of gambling only. You have to keep it totally separate and deal with it as if it didn't even exist. Since we are not kids, I think you are able to decide how to separate it from the rest of your money. Never forget that your bankroll is cash. Cash that you have already that you do not need for any other purpose. Your bankroll is not your credit card, nor any kind of checks received from the government, nor is it your Christmas bonus. Least of all, it is not a loan.

Consider your current bankroll of 200 units. Out of this, bring 20 units to the table and your initial (smallest) bet is one unit.

Your actual bankroll	**200**	**units**
Take to the table	**20**	**units**
Initial (smallest) bet	**1**	**unit**

It is simple, isn't it? Sure. You have only <u>one</u> thing to do. Keep yourself to it!

<u>Do not confuse the reason with the result</u>: The bankroll is not decided by the minimum bet, but we will decide the minimum bet according to our bankroll. In other words: you do not decide which table you want to play at, and take money with yourself according to it. Your money (existing bankroll) decides at which table you can play (which table can you "afford"). Never ever let yourself be diverted from your intentions!

If you don't have adequate bankroll, it will always be on your mind that "They can knock me out at any second—how can I continue [without money]?" With this type of thought in your mind, it is impossible to play. Losing sessions are a totally natural part of the game. It is just not acceptable that the above-mentioned thought comes into your mind and reduces your energy just because one or two losses happen. The established betting ratio guarantees that you will always be able to play under appropriate circumstances, assuring that you do not have to worry about losing sessions.

Here is how I define **money management**, and how I use it:

Manage your money in such a manner that there will always be a sufficient bankroll available in order to be able to make money again.

The inadequate bankroll / initial bet ratio is the most important reason why the majority of people leave the casino's battlefield as a loser.

It is an everyday practice in the casinos that when the busiest time comes, especially on weekends, they increase the table minimum. This is understandable. This is a business. If something is marketable at a higher price, why not do it? You don't have to participate. You do not have to be a customer. With the increased table minimum, a substantial number of players are forced to play with a higher bet, which is not permitted by their bankroll (if they have one at all).

They are **overbetting**. If somebody is overbetting, he has no control over his money. Overbetting is the surest way to the poorhouse. Do not let the casino control <u>your</u> money! If you cannot find a spot suitable for your bankroll, do not play! This is the only defense against overbetting (or the equivalent, against a sure loss).

Surely, you must have seen players who—since other tables are not available—jump into the $25 minimum table with $200. The $200 is just simply not enough to be at the $25 table. They are playing below the adequate bankroll. If we add to that the fact that many of them are betting only by their feelings, then undoubtedly they will not be making the winning group of players grow.

Allow me to mention a few more examples of unacceptable money management. We can observe on numerous occasions where players will raise their bets in multiples very quickly, sometimes even tenfold. Of course we are not talking about card counters, but about players who are betting by their feelings. They may win more hands than they lose, but they will ultimately still leave the battlefield as a loser.

You must have come across many players who buy-in to a $10 table with $20–$30, or to a $25 table with $50–$100. I feel sorry for them. If only I were the casino owner, these are the players that I would send a limo for—every day. They are the sure losers, because they are playing with a short (unacceptable) bankroll, which is one of the most important factors, after the lack of self-control, for a loss.

They will blame everybody in the casino, except themselves. They don't have money management skills.

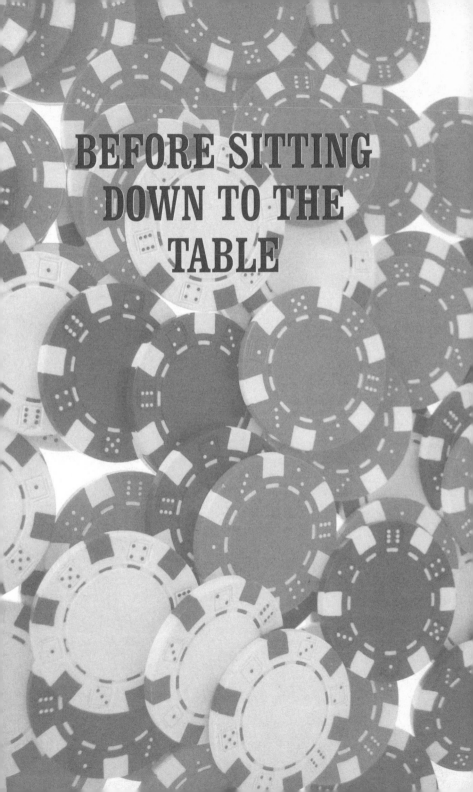

BEFORE SITTING DOWN TO THE TABLE

Be READY to Play

(If you're tired and don't play, you won't miss anything other than your lost money if you play when you're not prepared.)

I firmly believe that "to be ready to play" is one of the most important factors.

Did you travel to the casino for an hour in your car? Maybe. You think you are not tired, so let's go and play—you don't want to waste your time. Don't do it. I'm not saying you are tired physically probably, but to be fit only physically is not enough. You have to also be prepared mentally before you take action. To be prepared mentally is one of the most important things when we are talking about playing blackjack. To be "ready" to play means: being prepared physically <u>and</u> mentally.

To be prepared physically means you cannot be tired and your body has to be ready to play at least 3–6 hours per day. If you feel tired or sleepy, stop playing. You can start playing again when you are fully recovered. Many people think they have to be in the action always because they will "miss" something. You will not miss anything. All those casinos will be there tomorrow, and the day after tomorrow. You will never miss anything, only your lost money if you play when you are not prepared.

You do not have to run into a casino and start playing after a few minutes. If you see a busload of tourists coming in, let them go first. They don't have a lot of time to lose their money. To jump into the game right away is an attitude of the losers. They go into the casino, and they immediately lose a couple of hundred dollars. They pledge they will never come to a casino again, which usually means about 1–2 weeks. The majority do not part from casinos in a very good mood. I can understand them; losing is not good! However, this is the way most people play (gamble) week after week, year after year. This could be fine for some people, if they actually like to play (and lose) this way. But now I'm talking about <u>YOU</u>.

You have just arrived. Are you ready? No. Even if you have just driven an hour, you have to prepare yourself for the game. "Cool down!" Take a short walk, "discover" the casino even if you are there for the thousandth time, go to the washroom, look around—maybe a couple of friends are there. Acclimate to the circumstances. Take it easy. Get ready to play.

If the above mentioned are true when you have driven barely an hour to the casino, then they are true to an increased degree when you have traveled many hours by plane or bus! You need even more time to be ready for the game. Check in, have a meal, look around, and if it's too late, it is not necessary to play during the first night. Blackjack is an emotional game even if you are ready. But if you aren't? You need concentration and you have to be able to control your emotions. If you just jump in, you control nothing.

I hope you get the idea that you need to be "ready." **You have to be ready for the game before you sit down to the table**. Take your time. Focus on your game before you start to play. Think one more time about what is important: why you are playing, how long you want to play, the amount of your current bankroll, what the initial bet will be, etc. You have to be there totally.

You also have to be ready from a patience point of view. Just as a hunter would when he's hunting. If the hunter doesn't have the patience to wait for his prey, then he's not a good (winning) hunter. If *you* don't have the patience to sit and wait for the proper moment (when the table turns in your favor and a winning streak develops), then *you* cannot be a winning player.

Never forget: if you are not ready, you do not have patience. If you don't have patience, you don't have self-control. Without self-control, there is no way to win.

The CROWDED CASINO Is Not for You

(The goal of playing blackjack is not to get action.)

You just walked into the casino and it's a Saturday evening. In most casinos, this is the busiest time. It's not easy to see an empty spot at the tables.

You will see a lot of players who are willing to line up in order to get a spot to play. Some of them (mostly at the lower table minimum) will ask, "Is there a waiting list?" Let them play. They are the losers.

Think about it. Is it not silly to ask for a waiting list? They are asking nothing more than ". . . where can I lose my money?" Only the losers want to play at any price. They are desperate to play, or as I say, they are desperate to lose.

The goal of playing blackjack is not to get action. The goal is to make money. It is hard to make money anyway, but it is much harder if you do not feel comfortable. Do not jump into a game just because you are there.

Avoid a crowded table. Leave this situation for the weak players. They love to play there. Why? They make (too many) mistakes. At a crowded table, they have company. They are going to the casino for a different reason. They want to have a good time. They are right. Everybody wants to have a good time. They forget a very important fact. It is not easy to have a good time if you lose. If the casino is crowded, you cannot get the best circumstances and it is much "easier" to be a loser.

I would like to show you <u>how *not* to choose</u> a place to play. Let's look at a scenario. You just entered the casino and it's crowded. You would like to play, but it is almost impossible to get an open spot. Then, you spot a gentleman who has only two chips in front of him. You stand behind him, and on his next hand, he loses a double and is about to leave the table because he lost all of his money. You are happy to get a spot and jump into this position at the game.

Is this really the way to start to play? Yes, it is . . . for a loser. But not for you.

The casino must be large enough so that there should always be a seat where you can sit down in case you want to change tables. This criteria can be met even in a smaller casino if you are not playing during the "rush hours."

Sometimes, a big casino is insufficient if it doesn't allow you the possibility of changing tables without having to wait for a seat.

There must be enough tables with betting limits <u>corresponding to **your** bankroll</u>. Suppose your initial bet is $10. There are only $15 or higher open spots available. That casino is not for you at that particular time. If you sit down, you are overbetting. One of the surest ways to be a loser.

Look for the tables that suit your bankroll. Learn how many empty spots there are, first of all, at the tables where you want to play. If the availability is not sufficient, wait—maybe later it will be better. If you cannot get the best circumstances, don't play!

In closing, I have to say that, disregarding when I first started playing blackjack, I have never played on either Saturday or Sunday nights due to the points that I just laid out. During these nights, it is not always easy to find a suitable spot even at the $100 tables. I won't even mention the $25 tables which, during these busy periods, turn into the smallest minimum tables and do not secure an ideal environment required for optimum play.

If you add to this the increased volume of people during the evening hours who come to see different shows offered by the casinos, then it's easy to understand why it's not recommended to play during these busy times.

If the only chance you get to play is during the weekend, then try for the morning or early afternoons and leave the evenings to the losers.

In short, <u>do not play if the casino is too crowded</u>.

CHARTING a Table: Why It's Important

(If you don't want to chart a table, it's better not to play at all.)

In the chapter "Be Ready To Play," we talked about how you shouldn't jump into the game when you have just arrived at the casino. Before you make a decision where you want to play, you have to chart the tables in order to get the best possible circumstances for your game.

Charting a table is a good opportunity to cool down and to get ready to play after your arrival. It is also a must in order to try to find the best possible table where you want to play. You cannot underestimate the significance of charting, but in no way can you (or should you) exaggerate it.

Charting a table means to choose the best possible table for you. The most important is to only take into consideration tables which are suited for your bankroll. You will notice that it is not especially easy to find lower limit tables that suit your bankroll.

Some authors even suggest charting 12–15 tables. I would like to ask these authors how this can be possible outside of a Vegas-sized establishment, seeing as how many given casinos only have a total of 15 open tables to start with. Even if they have this number of open tables, it uses too much unnecessary time. Even if we only spend 3 to 4 minutes for each table, this already takes up about an hour. I have doubts that anyone, especially an average Joe, will (or should) spend this much time charting. And it's certainly not a sure bet that you will find the right one since a full hour has passed and anything could have changed.

Here is how I chart the tables:

A winning table is always a noisy table, loaded with happy people and most of the time with a lot of chips in front of them.

In most cases it is not easy to find an empty seat at a winning table, so if you find one, don't think twice. Jump in if any seats are available.

If you cannot find such a table, then try to check and concentrate primarily on the dealer's upcard at possible tables. The final hand total of the dealer does not matter. All of our decisions (the use of basic strategy) depend on the dealer's upcard, thus it's only natural that we want to play at a table where the dealer shows a weak upcard.

A dealer is	**weak**	if his upcard is	4, 5, 6
	neutral		2, 3, 7, 8
	strong		9, 10, J, Q, K, Ace

I do not find it necessary to chart more than 5–6 hands, since an average shoe in a 6–8 deck game with 5–7 players is 12–15 hands/shoe. The 5–6 hands gives almost the half of the shoe, and it doesn't make sense to chart one table for more than half a shoe. If the majority of the dealer's upcard show a strong dealer (9 or higher), keep walking. If it is neutral or weak, then we can get in on the action. It is possible that once you sit in on a game, the cards will turn, but at least you didn't start betting against a dealer's winning streak. If we do not join a table based on this, then we have a *minimum* 50% chance of jumping into a "hot table" (where the dealer is strong), which we simply do not need or want.

What can we expect from the dealer's upcard? From the possible 52 cards, there are 20 picture cards and aces which means 38% of the time (20 divided by 52) the dealer will show an ace or a face card. If we add to this the 9 (also a strong card for the dealer), then this is 24 cards out of 52—which represents 46% (when the dealer is strong). This is close to half of the possibilities. Thus, if we chart 6 hands at a table, we can expect a 9 or higher card to show up three times.

To me, it is always acceptable if out of 5–6 charted hands, the dealer gets a strong upcard twice. Most of the time, we cannot expect much better than this.

Charting a table is not the most exciting part of the game but an absolute must. If you don't want to chart a table, it's better not to think about playing blackjack at all.

You may ask the question, "What happens after charting 5–6 tables and spending 25–30 minutes and not finding a suitable table?" The answer is very simple—just like I said in an earlier chapter, a crowded casino is not for you!

If you are not able to find a suitable table, do not play. The tables will be there in an hour and will still be there tomorrow.

If you enter a casino that is relatively crowded and you find an empty table with a dealer standing behind it, this dealer is usually the one who has "cleaned" all the players out of their money. Definitely—even if you like to play head on head—don't sit down to this table except if the table is just about to open and nobody has played yet. If you ask a dealer standing behind an empty table, "Did you just open up?" you will get an honest answer most of the time. If the answer is, "It was open already," then avoid that table.

Let me mention one more thing. When you come across and play a hand-dealt game, it's very important that the game be safe (cheat-free). There are two really simple indications of a safe game.

First is an *apprentice dealer*. An apprentice dealer doesn't have enough experience to know how to cheat, and without a doubt, you will get an honest game.

An apprentice dealer is recognizable by the following: slow dealing, usually a floorperson stands behind him, he repeats the rules out loud—exactly how he was trained (for example, in the case of double down, he says, "One card only").

Second, the table is winning. If you find such a table, stop charting right away and sit down as fast as you can as this is what you are looking for. This type of table will fill up very quickly.

I can confirm through personal experience what various surveys state—it's hardest to play against an older male or female dealer (over forty-five) and it's the easiest against a young female who is under thirty. Take this fact into consideration if you find two similar (good) tables.

If possible, avoid dealers who are visibly in a bad mood because you don't want their negativity to rub off on you and be detrimental to *your* emotions. It's not good to be around negative people.

You Must Develop SELF-CONTROL

(Self-control is not your defense against a big win;
it's a defense against a big loss.)

Why do you think the casinos and websites do not write about self-control when explaining how to play the game? Because this is what really puts them in peril! A player with good discipline, who has an enormous amount of self-control, is much more dangerous than a perfect card counter.

To learn the basic strategy is the easier and simpler half of the game. While the basic skills are relatively easy to master, it's the "intangibles" that separate the winners from the losers. It's probably no surprise that one of those intangibles is self-discipline, which all of us lack from time to time and situation to situation. The other half is more difficult and takes much more time to master. We are not talking about material knowledge, but about the kind of things that affect us from the inside. To control these things is much more difficult than achieving the material knowledge. It is much easier to learn, for example, if you have 13 and the dealer shows a 6, you stand, than it is to follow your intelligence instead of your emotions under real casino conditions.

To control your game is at least as important as all the other material. These make up the other 50% of what it takes to become a winning player. Please do not underestimate the importance of these factors. These are as important as anything else. If you don't take your time to learn them and don't employ them in the everyday casino routine, then you have no chance of being a winner.

As a matter of fact, the basic strategy is not a choice from a "what" or "how" to decide point of view. It's written (in the basic strategy) what you have to follow. Thus, this doesn't really distinguish between being successful or unsuccessful, since you just have to follow set rules.

Take it easy. You cannot gamble in a rush! <u>Plan your time</u>. You cannot be in the situation that, if for whatever reason, you have to leave in an hour or less and you say, "Okay let's go to the casino and play one more quick session." With that suggestion, you are suggesting to yourself nothing but "Let's win quickly," since there is no good reason to suppose you want to lose quickly. But we know there is no way to win quickly. Then why would you spend only this single hour? This is not the style of a serious winning player. Leave it for the losers.

How many times have you read or heard from authors that they just "dropped in" for an hour for a session? What kind of self-control is this?

If you are with your husband, girlfriend, et al., there is one more really good reason to plan your time. You don't want to get in any kind of argument as to when you should go for dinner or leave the casino—which does not help you to concentrate on your game.

Without a game plan, the game (the casino!) will control you rather than you controlling the game!

If you know all the rules, how the game is played, how to play the game, what you can expect from the game, when to quit, how to manage your money, and so on, it is now "only" up to you to follow them. You know what you <u>have</u> to do, but doing it is quite another matter. To beat the casino is a tough battle. The toughest battle you face is with yourself. <u>The deal is</u> not between you and the casino. It is <u>between you and yourself</u>. Knowing all the rules means nothing if you lack self-control—you will remain a loser. You have to have your emotions under control, or otherwise you cannot beat the house. <u>You have to control the game and not let the game control you</u>! You must have confidence in yourself, and you cannot allow yourself to be influenced by anybody else or by any circumstances. Something always will happen around you. The casino is not a "quiet nunnery." You have to be able to concentrate on your own play regardless of what is going on around you. This is a must, and that's why you need self-knowledge. You must act according to your self-knowledge!

Do not let yourself be charmed.

Do not underestimate the people who run casinos. They are very good businessmen. Their job is to separate you from your money, and they do their job well. They know all the tricks. They want you to play on <u>their</u> conception, not on yours. They want you not to think about money. In order to do this, they provide polite service, use chips rather than cash, no clock, free drinks, free food, loud music, a laid-back atmosphere, a gourmet dinner, entertainment, gifts, etc., and they use all the tricks that you can imagine to make you comfortable and happy and otherwise distracted from your goal. Casinos create all the conditions, all of which have the sole purpose of diverting your attention from one thing— you are there to make money. The casinos try to relieve you from your money in the most painless way. If you want to be a winner, you must become aware of the effects of the above and only let those affect you that don't fundamentally influence your actions.

If these strategies have an influence on you, you are still not mentally prepared. Mental preparation and self-control are much more than 50% of the game. The majority of the players are not prepared mentally and have no self-control. That's why more than 95% are losers. To acquire a basic knowledge of the game is the easiest part of the preparation, but to be ready means to be ready mentally and physically. You must be ready in the sense that your self-control is working. This takes a much longer time. Sometimes it takes years, and you have to work on it.

Every time you act differently from what you know you should do, recognize these as the problems that you have to change. <u>Your self-control is the most important thing</u>. I define self-control according to the following: if you are capable of following everything that you know, and you play according to it, then you have self-control.

I interpret self-control as: if I know with my intelligence what I have to do in order to be a winner, then I will not act in a different way in the casino, guided by my "bad emotions," and let myself be influenced by the casino's circumstances. **Self-control is nothing more than following the rules that you already know.** I know that to say this is a hundred times easier than it is to follow it. The most important thing that separates the winning players from the losing ones is self-control.

How can you develop a perfectly working self-control? If any doubts arise, pose the following questions to yourself: Is this what I really have to do? Or is this just my self-control not working? Is what I want to do harmonized with what I know (with my goals, with my game plan, and with everything else that I know)? Is this really what I have to do in this situation? "Put a brake on yourself" if you want to do something that is unsuitable. Say to yourself, "I am capable of not doing it." Let's say that your bankroll allows a $20 initial bet. You are looking around the casino, and there isn't anything else but a couple of good tables with a minimum bet of $25. At one of them, the play isn't even going too badly for the players. The little devil inside of you says, "Sit down. Sit down and play." You stop, maybe check out a few hands. But don't sit down and play. Get it? Do—not—sit—down—and—play. You know you still cannot afford that table. If you don't sit down, if you walk: *now this is self-control!*

<u>Do not let yourself become emotionally involved in the game.</u> Don't be too excited about winning or losing. To be emotionally involved is dangerous in and of itself, but it is crucial if you are losing. If you feel you cannot control your emotions, stop playing! Take your time. Just like in any sport, if the team is getting blown out, the coach calls a time out. Be your own coach. Your self-control has to work. It will just sometimes happen that you lose what you brought to the table. Do not try to recover your losses by reaching into your pocket. The recovery never comes. Lots of people who are losing figure they are "due" to win, but winning is never due. When they are losing, they are on streak. They are betting on a streak. But why bet on a losing one? Do not chase your losses because they will catch you (emotionally) before you catch them. Get up and walk. Get it? Get—up—and—walk. Everybody knows that the first loss is the cheapest. *Now this is self-control!*

<u>You have to accept the importance of self-control.</u> I could also say that you need to develop the kind of attitude that is realistic. This is the biggest single factor that makes the difference between losers and winners. Without a doubt, you have heard stories about someone sitting down with $20 and, in a short period of time, turning it into

$2,000. It happens, and it will happen again. But this is not typical. Those who tell these stories are convinced that you have to go for a big win. The majority of the people in the casinos <u>think</u> about the big win. I would rather say, they are <u>dreaming</u> about the big win. Stop dreaming. If you want to dream, do not go in the casino. This is not the place to dream. Dreamers are losers. You can like or dislike what I'm telling you, but go back to the reality. It is just not realistic, for instance, to try to double or triple your starting stake. People who believe they can start with a few bucks and end up winning thousands of dollars just lost complete track of reality.

<u>If you don't have self-control</u> (or you are not able to develop it), if you cannot overcome and control (or discipline) yourself in every situation, and if you don't have patience to wait for the best opportunity, then you will never be able to beat the casino. Blackjack is not the type of game where you can drop in to the casino with a small amount of money and promptly make big money. If this is your goal, try something else. Don't play blackjack. One important reason why people lose is they don't attach importance to the fact that you have to control the game.

<u>Self-control</u> is not your defense against a big win; it <u>is a defense against a big loss</u>. So propose this question to yourself: "Do I have self-control?" If you are honest, I would bet you that your answer will be "Maybe not perfectly yet,

or not at all." Maybe it takes a year or two. But if you don't get it, if you don't have it, go for it. Without it, you will never be a part of the proud team of winners.

PLAYING AT THE TABLE

Go with the STREAK

(Bet with the streak or do not bet at all.)

How many times have you heard, when the dealer shows an ace and is asking for insurance, somebody say, "There is no face on the table, so it's almost a sure blackjack," and he buys insurance. There is no question about it—if there is no face card on the table, there is a better chance that the dealer will have it.

However, just because no face cards are shown, we cannot draw the conclusion that the next card will be a face.

The streak is that no picture cards are showing, and we have to suppose the streak is going to continue.

The streaks (we can call them "trends" as well) are a very important part of gambling and a big factor that, most of the time, determine the winner.

Certainly you've already met people who think, if something happens, the opposite is due to occur. Nothing says that something is due. Sticking to the example we just mentioned, a picture card is not due just because we haven't seen any.

For instance, if they have 16 against the dealer's 10, and previously there were three small cards, then in most of the cases (after a long thought process), they will nervously gesture to the dealer that they do not want any additional cards.

They think that after three small cards, one big card is due. By thinking like this, they have already made multiple mistakes. First of all, as we know, standing on 16 against a 10 is the biggest mistake. Second, they're betting against the trend. They suppose a big card after three small cards would mean the turning of the trend. We never bet against a trend.

It is a well-known example from roulette that if three consecutive black numbers came up, then—if someone wants to "jump" into the game anyway—obviously they have to bet on black and not red only because they think that red is due. (If you want to jump into a game of roulette anyway [whatever happens], it is best to wager on black *after* the first black number. In case the trend turns around, we bet on the wrong side only once.)

Translating the above into the game of blackjack, losses and wins come in streaks. Most of the time, one win does not follow one loss, but rather two, three, four, or (rarely) longer winning or losing streaks follow each other. Nobody can explain why these streaks occur and when. Regardless, these are the facts.

Trends—losing or winning—happen at every table, in every casino, all the time. There is no such thing that says it's time to turn over or it's time for a losing trend to come to an end. Losing streaks could last for hours. You don't have to be a part of it. If a losing streak occurs, just leave the table.

How can you profit from this fact?

The "bet with the trend" in blackjack means that if a winning streak develops at a table, then keep playing at that table; however, never get caught in a situation where you have raised your initial bet 4, 5, or 10 times. Betting with the streak does not necessary mean you have to increase your bet with an unnecessary big step. Merely because one winning streak occurs, you don't have to escalate your bet too rapidly. Just keep betting because if you keep increasing your bet, then sooner or later you will always lose the biggest bet.

It's quite often seen at the $25 table that someone will increase their bet to $100–$200, sometimes even to $300–$500. In the majority of cases, they will leave the casino as a loser. Why? Because this is not money management. If a winning trend occurs, your money management skills still have to work, since one of the most important things you need to do to beat the dealer is manage your money. If you increase your bet by disregarding your bankroll, then in the previous example, a $25 bet will increase to $200. A $200 bet requires a minimum $4,000 bankroll. Most of these players don't have this amount of money. They are simply overbetting. Eight times your initial bet—just because there's a winning trend—is just not justifiable.

A three or longer winning streak very rarely develops. As I explained my betting method in my first book (*The Most Powerful Blackjack Manual*), regardless of the enormity of the winning streak, I do not increase my initial bet by more than three times. I do not rely on winning more than six hands in a row. I can understand those who after winning three or even two hands in a row will decrease the size of their bet (regression of the bet).

If a long winning streak doesn't develop (and in the majority of cases, it won't), then we can achieve a bigger profit with regression. The bets will follow in sequence such that the third or fourth bet will always be smaller than the first two. It's true that if you win more hands in a row, the profit will be smaller, but since long winning streaks rarely develop (7 or more winning hands in a row), the long term will show slightly more winnings. You will never lose your biggest bet, which (if it happens during a split and double) can negatively affect your emotions.

Surely you notice the crowd at the slot machines. Whoever knows me knows I'm not the biggest fan of the slots—just like any other guy who plays blackjack. Why? The slot players try to overcome an average house advantage of about 10%. They're trying to do the impossible.

If anybody is gambling and it's not permitted to manage your money, then the most important factor (contributing to your win) has been taken away. This exact thing happens at a slot machine.

In the majority of casino games, when the odds are in your favor, you are able to increase your bet. You are able to manage your money. You can't do the same thing with the slots. If somebody tries to challenge the slots, they are going to go broke. It's not enough that you are playing against a 10% house advantage; you are also not able to manage your money.

That's why I'm not a fan of the slots. You can *try* to pull a million with twenty bucks, but that's about it.

How can you identify a losing streak? If you lose three or more hands in a row, then this is already a sufficient indication that you are in losing streak. As for me, if this happens, I take a break (i.e., walk to the washroom, talk to others, have a coffee, etc.). I then come back to the table and take one more chance. But if I lose two (max three) hands again, I just get up and leave the table.

I'm sure you must have sat at a $10 table when somebody buys in $100. After losing the entire sum in a very short period of time, this player laughingly states, "What a hot table." He then proceeds to buy in another $100 and keeps playing. He probably didn't realize that it was a bad streak. What a loser. Do not be a part of the losers. Bet with the streak or do not bet at all.

Don't Worry about
OTHERS AT THE TABLE

(Should I say, ignore them?)

When you're playing at a table, naturally you'll meet completely different types of characters. I'm not saying to ignore them, but I say don't worry about them at all. Consider this from the following two viewpoints:

1. Don't worry about the way they play.
2. Ignore the remarks that come your way every now and then.

The remarks of another player cannot influence you, because you must know that a player who makes these comments is a weaker player than you. We know this because if they weren't weaker, then they wouldn't be making those comments to begin with.

You will always meet <u>the teacher-type player</u>, who wants to teach everyone what to do. Most of the time you'll realize that their chips will disappear much faster than anybody else's. Nobody really cares to hear what a good player they are, just like nobody cares about you. Never ever try to teach or explain any kind of decision to any other player. If you try to do such a thing, your only accomplishment will be decreasing your mental readiness.

It seems to me that for some reason, there are a few things in the basic chart that a large percentage of people "forget" to learn.

If you have soft 18 (A, 7), many players (not only beginners) would never think to hit against a face. For them, it seems to be a good hand. However, the odds are against them. You will see (just like how with a hard 12, you hit against a 2) almost every time you hit a soft 18, some players will cast a scornful look at you. Probably they don't understand what you're doing. Don't even try to explain. Your decision is the right one. It is more than enough that you know. Just play your game. (It's true that if we hit, we will lose a lot of hands; however, if we stand, we will lose even more.)

Many times the following has happened to me. Playing as anchor, I hit a 12 against a deuce, get a face and somebody starts to "teach" me right away—since they are an "expert." (If somebody claims they are an expert, it is the surest sign that they aren't.)

"What are you doing?" they ask.

What is even worse is if after that the dealer pulls an 8 on his 13.

How can I tell them, "Hey, I wrote a book already about this issue, you should read it"? In the same situation, if I get the 8 and after that the dealer busts with a face card, I'm the best anchor in the world. Just don't be <u>too</u> proud of ourselves.

Of course, since there is a chance to bust, sometimes it will happen. When you do bust, don't have any doubts that you made the right decision. Occasionally there will be somebody who tries to "protect" you. "Don't worry about it, sir"—you made the right decision. He is teaching. He laughs at you like an accomplice, making you aware that he "knows" too.

The casino is not a school.

It's not a good idea to advise other players who you don't know. If they end up losing their hand after they took your advice, they will probably hold a grudge against you and let you know that your advice doesn't mean much. After all, you cannot teach anybody with a few tidbits of advice anyway, so there is no good reason to allow yourself to be shaken from your serenity.

To show how hopeless it is to teach anybody at the table, allow me to tell you one story from my personal experience. A middle-aged woman sat down next to me, and after a couple of hands, I realized that she was a beginner.

She said to me, "This is the second time I have ever played."

My next hand was a 12 against the dealer's 2, to which I hit, of course.

The lady asked me, "Is this the right decision?"

"Yes," I said.

Out of pure luck, on the next hand she got a 12 against the dealer's 5. Without any questions, she asked for another card, which was a 9.

The dealer got a picture card in the hole and a 5 after that, to which the lady proudly exclaimed, "I made the right decision, didn't I?"

What could I say? How could I start teaching her there?

I just replied, "Ma'am, when you win, it's always the right decision."

<u>Everybody who is playing has as much right to play as you do.</u> They not only have the right to play, but they have the right to play the way that suits them. We do not have the right to criticize other players at the table just because of the way they play. Just like in other aspects of life, we have to respect others next to us. I have learned to keep my mouth shut to the point that I don't criticize anybody just because they made a certain decision. If you are not able to tolerate others, you can get up and leave the table.

It's generally true that if you move to a table with a higher minimum required bet (if your bankroll allows), there will be fewer unskilled players. Generally at the higher minimum tables, you will meet better players. However, this is true only "generally" because a higher bettor doesn't necessarily mean a better player. Sometimes it just means a higher bettor. If I had here in front of me the number of chips representing how many times I have met a weaker-than-average player at the $50 table, it would be a very nice sum of money.

Many players think that the <u>decisions of the anchor</u> affect the whole table. Is it true? Yes; however, it is just as true as how any other player's decision affects the whole table. We always remember who made the last "mistake." I know it would be nice to have a good player at the anchor, but it would be just as nice to have a good player in every seat. But this is not reality. The majority of the people don't even have an idea of what they're doing. The decision of the anchor doesn't have any greater effect than any of the other players'. It is, in itself, very hard to find a table where, sooner or later, one or more weak players don't appear. You have to try to accustom yourself to this fact.

If you cannot put this behind you, you will just stress yourself out. DO NOT EVEN TRY TO TEACH anybody at the table. Since weak players don't know too much, they will start to pick on you sooner or later. Most of the time, sooner.

None of the other player's decisions—including the anchor—have an effect on your overall success. Therefore, keep in mind **what the other players are doing at the table is not your business.** They cannot do anything for, or against, you.

Don't Play Any SIDE BETS
(Including Insurance)

(If you see somebody taking a side bet,
you are watching a loser.)

From time to time, casinos will offer many types of rules on top of the regular ones. The game goes on as usual, but the player can make an additional bet, the side bet. This side bet is completely independent from the original bet and has nothing to do with the original bet.

Many variations of blackjack have come and gone through the years.

The variations are endless. Some examples are:

- Match the dealer—You get paid if your first card matches with the dealer.
- Perfect pair—You have to have a pair. If suited, you win more.
- Lucky ladies—You win if the first two cards' total equals 20. If you get a pair of queen of hearts, you win the most.
- Blackjack jackpot—The casino will give you the opportunity to win a large progressive jackpot for a side bet.
- Four aces—You get paid if your first four cards are aces.
- The list goes on . . .

I don't want to go into detailed analysis of these since it can be very easily proven that any of these side bets are extremely disadvantageous for the player. Needless to say, they are favorable to the casino—which is why they offer them. Just like at the slots, you can have a lot of fun, and if you are lucky, you can win, but in the long term, these are definitely losing bets.

I will demonstrate with one simple example as to why these side bets are so unfavorable to the player. One type of side bet is the Lucky Seven (the name could be different from casino to casino). You get paid if you have one, two, or three 7s as your first, second, and third cards. The payout will be different if the second and the third 7s are suited or unsuited. For a one-dollar side bet for the first 7, you get paid (usually) three dollars. The real odds of getting a 7 as a first card are 1:13 and you get paid 1:3. If you get two 7s, you get paid fifty dollars, but the real odds are 1:169 . . .

Should I continue?

Let me talk about **a special side bet, the insurance**.

I must begin by saying that the insurance wager is generally a bad bet for the player! The insurance is offered only if the dealer's upcard is an ace. You can insure your hand against the dealer's blackjack—against the possibility of the dealer having been dealt a 10-value card as a hole card. Many players think that they are insuring a good hand, but let's make it very clear that we don't actually get any insurance. We are not insuring anything. We are making a side bet.

In fact, what the players are betting on is whether or not the dealer's hole card is a 10-value card. Therefore, the name *insurance* is misleading. Since the casinos allow you to make an additional bet, if the dealer's upcard is an ace, the dealer should ask, "Does anyone want to bet that I will have a blackjack by having a 10-value hole card?"

If the dealer has a blackjack and you don't, you lose your original bet. However, your insurance bet wins your bet back. The bet is referred to as *insurance* because, if the dealer has a blackjack and the player doesn't, the insurance bet "saved" the player's original bet. Note that the insurance bet has nothing to do with the original bet. Regardless of the side bet, the original bet is won or lost in the usual way.

We have to talk about a **special circumstance**, where the player has blackjack and the dealer's upcard is an ace. Should we insure our own blackjack? (Should we make a side bet?)

We shouldn't. Why? Because the odds are against us. The dealer will have blackjack 4 times out of 13 (four 10-value cards of the total 13 - 30.8%) and will not have blackjack 9 times out of 13 (69.2%). So if we don't take even money, we will not win 4 times, but otherwise we make 50% more.

Have you ever thought about the fact that, when and if it comes to the insurance bet, the casino never puts up any money? If the player loses, the dealer takes the insurance bet. If the player wins, the dealer pays with the player's own money. It's a good trick, isn't it?

I have to tell you that the insurance bet is not only one of the most confusing bets for a rookie, but one of the most arguable bets of the game. When it comes to taking this bet, even the biggest experts are completely divided on opinions. Only one thing is sure: never take insurance on weak hands (less than 19).

As for me, it is hard to tolerate, emotionally, having the best hand and not making any money. I am guaranteed to win an equal amount of my bet. However, many experts would say it this way: "I am guaranteed to win less." I never take insurance unless I have a blackjack. If you don't want to take even money, I will not blame you. Play your game. From a percentage perspective, you'll be correct.

All of the side bets are favorable for the house. After all, that's why they've been introduced. The casinos usually introduce them in order to initiate players (mostly novices) to the game. Let them play. <u>I strongly suggest</u> that you never play these options, and <u>never take a side bet!</u>

Should You Go for the BIG WIN?

***(Players who go for the big win next day usually don't
even have enough money to go to the casino.)***

There is not much to say about those who run into a casino
with the preconceived notion that they will double their
money and/or win a few hundred/thousand dollars. We can
forget about them. They are the losers.

Aside from them and the many different betting
variations, there are basically two different gambling
philosophies:

1. The first is the solid approach—or we can call it the conservative way—which goes for achieving a relatively smaller win in accordance with the initial bet. As soon as we make a profit, we can make a decision based on what we have talked about already (i.e., expectations, self-control). This approach requires a lot of time, a very big dose of patience, and fantastic self-control. If you don't possess these, then this approach is not for you.

2. The second is what I call "Go for the big win." How does this work?

Here is an example. For simplicity, let's assume an initial bet of $10. You sit down to the table with $200. After a relatively short period of time, you are up $100 (which is 10 units). Now you make the decision. Let's go for the big kill! In order to go for the big kill, you have to increase your initial bet substantially. Let's take a modest increase

where you increase your initial bet from $10 to $25. This in itself is not a big bet, but it is two and a half times your original. This increased amount, by the way, is also not enough for the big kill, but you have two possibilities:

A. If at the very beginning you get a split situation with a double on one hand—and it loses—you are out $75, which is 7.5 times your original initial bet. One bet easily wiped out almost everything that you worked to achieve in the last hour or so. If you keep making the same bet ($25), it's easy to lose your initial bankroll in a very short period of time since it's only 8 units (of your original $200). This is just not enough.

B. The other possibility is that you keep winning when you increase your bet to $25. For the real big win, sooner or later you will have to increase your $25 bet. Most of the time, the points written in A above will ensue.

In other words, when you are going for a big win most of the time, you increase your bet too early (if you start it too late, presumably the winning streak will end soon). Actually, what happens is that your increased bet (in comparison to your original bankroll) does not produce an adequate initial bet/bankroll ratio. Playing under these circumstances, as we know, leads to defeat. You are overbetting, which is the surest way to the poorhouse.

Note: there is another possibility. Instead of raising the initial bet, you can employ any kind of a progressive betting method (i.e., 10-10-15-20-25 or 10-10-15-15-20, etc.). I am convinced that by using this method, you can achieve some extra profit, but doubt that a big kill will ever result. I think that expecting more than 5–6 consecutive wins on a regular basis stands quite far from reality. Thus, with this method, it's hard to even imagine increasing your initial bet by fourfold.

So what is my answer to the question, "Go for a big kill or not?" I have to tell you that most of the time going for the big win just doesn't work. The majority of the players who go for the big win will find that the next day they don't have enough money to go for even a small win (or for that matter, to go to the casino at all).

You can go for it, but after you increase your bet and lose back the amount you originally won, drop down to the initial $10 bet. What's even better (if you got back to your original bankroll after losing *many* hands) is to call it a day. You can say, "I tried for the big kill, I had a chance, it didn't work out but at least I didn't lose. I broke even." Although the big kill eluded you and you lost the profit that you've already made once, at least you didn't lose more.

When you are playing in a casino, there will always be someone who bets more than you do, and such a player could be at any of the tables—including yours. High rollers might bet thousands of dollars on each hand, but don't be influenced by them. Play your own game and bet at your comfort level. If your bankroll allows a ten-dollar initial bet, you are a ten-dollar player. If your bankroll allows a fifty-dollar initial bet, you are a fifty-dollar player, and so on. If you are a twenty-five-dollar player, don't try to go for the big win with a two-hundred-dollar initial bet. It's just not going to work.

Remember, it's much better to be a hundred-dollar winner than a thousand-dollar loser. A small profit, after all, is better than no profit.

We are all different in life, so why would we be the same at the gambling table? The style of how we play could be conservative or aggressive. Some of us would like to be a tiger for one day rather than a sheep for a hundred years, and there is no question that it is much better to be a tiger than a sheep. But don't forget that even if we are a tiger, we are fighting against a giant. Of course, we can't knock out the giant, but we can get a piece of the pie!

In order to get it, don't fluctuate your initial bet. Stick to the initial bet that is indicated by your bankroll.

Don't Forget to QUIT on Time

(Only the good player knows how to quit as a loser
—before all of his money is gone.)

It's much easier to jump into the game than to quit. To quit is never easy. It is one of the most critical decisions that you have to make. Probably <u>the</u> most critical one. Right here, at the beginning, I have to make something very clear—there is no exact formula for when to quit. There is simply no way to set up a rigorous rule. Generally, I truly believe there is no reason to play by your feelings. However, if I want to make an exception, when to quit would be one of them.

Surely you have read many suggestions on how <u>authors determine</u> when to quit. (Examples: Move to another table if you lose three hands in a row, if you lose the first four hands in a session, when you have lost money on the shoe . . . and so on. The variations are endless.) All of these rules are set up arbitrarily. Maybe the best one states to quit when you are ahead. This sounds good, but I have two problems with it. First of all, it is too universal. Second, it will happen sometimes that you're never ahead.

In *The Most Powerful Blackjack Manual*, I went into much detail about when to quit. Without using my method, it's very tough to give detailed suggestions. Therefore, try to use the following in general.

When to quit is strongly influenced by <u>how frequently</u> you can play. If you have only two-three opportunities to play a year, it is almost impossible to come up with any idea of when to quit. You are probably not going to quit after two or three hours of play. I still say that if, after a few hours of playing, the number of winning sessions are fewer than the number of losing sessions, accept that this is not your day and quit for the day.

We have to take into consideration whether we are in a winning or in a losing situation before we make a decision about quitting a session. Let's talk about how to <u>quit as a winner and how to quit as a loser</u>. The rule that you employ can be simple, but to adhere to it is much harder. This is one of the most important factors that distinguish winning and losing players. A winning player always knows (always is able, since he/she has the self-control) how to quit as a loser.

Of course, during the game, you don't have to think about how to quit as a loser. If you keep losing, take a break and then continue. Give it one more chance. If you take a loss, the session is over. You are about to quit as a loser. Don't think about it. Get up and leave the table. Easy? Yes. Just do it.

Maybe it sounds stupid but you have <u>to learn to lose</u>. It doesn't matter how good a player we are, and it doesn't matter how successful we are—losing sessions are unavoidable from time to time. Nobody can guarantee such a system, method, scheme, or call it whatever you want, whereby we win all the time. We just try to win most of the time. Every time you leave the casino as a loser, think about which rule you broke. Sometimes it will happen that nothing could have helped. We lost and that's it. But if you made a mistake, remember it. Only the beginners and the weak players make the same mistake twice.

I would like to mention one more possibility, a circumstance when I recommend that a player quit even if he is a little bit down. <u>Stop playing when you've recouped losses</u>. Say you have been playing for a couple of hours on different tables and are down 20 units. Suddenly the cards

turn. You win one hand after the other. You just won back almost the entire 20 units and you're nearly even after a big loss. Then the cards turn again, and no more significant wins occur. Just lose one, win one, etc. It's going nowhere. Give it one more chance and quit.

To quit as a winner is a little bit different than quitting as a loser. It is only natural, you can say, since to quit as a winner is much more pleasant than to quit as a loser. To quit as a winner always depends on how much we won, since we don't want to quit a winning streak prematurely. In short, to quit as a winner is a little bit of an art.

There are two possibilities:

1. You are up but not a significant amount. Let's assume you play for about two and a half hours and won 7–8 units. Use your judgment and make a decision according to your circumstances. If you want you, can quit or you can play more. But as soon as you start

going south, just quit as a winner even if it's not a significant amount.

2. The win exceeds your starting money significantly. Let's assume that you start the game with 20 units. After two and a half hours of play, there are 50 units in front of you—thus showing a 30-unit profit. This is a significant profit! In this case, keep two things in mind:

   a. Do not quit a winning streak too soon just because you lost a few hands in a row.

   b. Unconditionally quit as a winner before you lose everything back.

We can accomplish these two conditions simultaneously with the <u>stop-loss method</u>. This method is known to stock or futures-market investors. The essence of the stop-loss is that, after a profit occurred, we fix the amount of profit that we will never allow to be lost back. I set this limit approximately at one-third of the profit. In other words, I do not allow myself to lose back more than one-third of my profits. If you keep winning, you should set up new stop-losses at approximately every 10 units. The stop-loss method is not applicable if you have not won enough money.

Set up your own limit, and keep yourself to it!

When you say (to yourself), "One more shoe [or hand]," after a few neutral ones, stick to it. One more can't mean two more! One means one. There will always be other opportunities. The tables will be there in an hour and will still be there tomorrow! Greed is what stops the majority of players from being able to quit on time. Don't be (too) greedy. Have self-control.

I would like to bring to your attention one more thing. Say you're playing at the $25 table and after a couple of hours you're up $200. You achieved this in such a way that you were never significantly down. I know it's not a tremendous amount of money and the majority of players who play at the $25 table truly believe that it is peanuts and not what they came for. It is 8 units. Believe me and learn that 8 units is not too small of a profit. In this situation, you have to start thinking about how to quit as a winner.

Think about this comparison. You're playing at the same table and lose about $200, but after a couple of hours, you recoup your losses and are now "going nowhere." You've come back 8 units. Give it one more chance and quit.

Do you realize the similarity but still a very big difference?

In the majority of the cases when the time comes to quit, you have to take into consideration where you've come back from. We have to know what the expectation is.

In the first case, you went from 0 to +8 units. In the second case, you went from—8 to 0 units. Many say, "Big deal, what's the difference?" I say, "A lot." Quitting from above (as a sure winner) or quitting from below (after a comeback) is just not the same. Not too many people think about such things, but these are the tiny details that make the difference between a winner and a loser.

ODDS & ENDS

16th SECRET

Instead of "YOU NEVER KNOW," Use "YOU ALWAYS KNOW"

(You "never know" in the short term, but you always "have to know" in the long term).

How many times have you heard at the table, "You just never know"?

I think this sentence is a bad excuse for people who really don't know what's going to happen—those who really don't know what to expect from the game.

It's true that you never know what will happen in the next split second, but this is not really important. However, using this excuse to keep playing at a hot table or staying on 16 hoping the dealer will bust on a face card is the attitude of losers.

Yes, you never know what the next card is going to be, but you know that the next card means nothing in and of itself.

Yes, you never know what will happen on a certain day or session, but you know what will happen in the long term. Therefore, if you hear, "You never know," you know you're listening to a weak player. You could continue the sentence with "You just never know what will happen in the next second." You just never know what the next card will be. But you always know what will happen in the long term. Although truly, you know what will happen in the short term as well (since you will lose more often than win by staying on 16 against the dealer's face card). There are only a few possibilities and you know that one of them will ultimately transpire.

Thus in reality you always know. You have a few different possibilities and the only thing you don't know is which one of these few possibilities will unfold at a given time.

Instead of saying "You never know," you should say, "You always know."

This in turn will also boost your self-confidence since you know what will happen. What you expect to happen will happen.

Surely it's happened to you many times after you left a table, you wondered what might have happened if you didn't leave the table at that moment. "I'll never know," you thought to yourself, but you always know that you had  only two options. Never ask yourself, "What could have happened?" You either would have won or you would have lost.

"Anything can happen" is nothing but the weak player's excuse for their insecurity. Instead of knowing what will happen, they try to philosophize that anything can happen and nothing depends on them.

In other words, the "anything can happen" attitude perilously steers you in a direction that everything depends on luck. However, luck doesn't affect your game in the long term. When you had only two choices, instead of "anything can happen," you made a decision and you chose one of them.

Never ever blame yourself and think about what could have happened if you chose the other option.

Yes, anything can happen to a weak player.

Yes, anything can happen to those who are not prepared for the game and for the expectations of the game.

The "anything can happen" is just as bad of an excuse as the "Can you believe this?"

You Don't Need a CREDIT CARD
in the Casino

*(Who do you think lines up at the bank
machines, the winners?)*

I never step into a casino thinking that today I will win
$100, $200, $1,000 (you can choose the amount), but with
the thought that I will win the "battle" again. I will beat
"them" (the intrepid giant) again, and this is what gives me
the reward (and the cash). The average person beating the
big business casino! This gives such a rewarding feeling that
nothing can compare to it. And the well-deserved reward

always shows itself as hard cash. Why should I need bank cards for this?

When you enter a casino, you can see bank machines everywhere. It's easy to find them. The casino wants to make sure that you have access to more money at any time. I'm sure you've seen (many times) people lining up at the cash machines. Were you in this line? Who do you think line up there? The winners? The winners don't need more money.

You have established your bankroll—you know how much you need when you enter the casino. Take the amount of money that is necessary according to your daily play plan. And that's it. If it's gone, it's gone. <u>You</u> decided what your daily plan is, and you had a good reason why you decided as you did. Don't deviate from what you decided. Stick to it. Don't let the casino's devil lead you astray and get you to line up for more cash.

Your bankroll is hard cash, and your credit card and any other bank cards are <u>not</u> part of your bankroll! If you have to lose, you have to lose. That's too bad in and of itself, but getting the bill a few weeks later? This is not a smart way to gamble. This is not the way that a winner manages their money. The "battle" is basically strictly for money, more accurately for cash. You do not need any kind of card for this "battle."

Not having bank cards with you is part of having self-control. *<u>We leave all of our credit and bank cards at home!</u>*

These kinds of cards don't have a place in a casino. When I talk about "bank cards," this also includes debit cards. Many players argue that they don't like taking large amounts of cash with them. I agree and I don't either. However, going to a casino has to be an exception to this.

Let me ask you something. Once you've made, for example, $2,000, do you want to deposit the money? Right in the casino? The vast majority of the machines in the casino do not even take deposits. You have to take the cash home. So what's the difference? Taking in cash or taking out cash? Nothing. You have to carry cash anyway.

Do not underestimate what I just told you. Many players do. They are the losers. I hope you don't think you need your bank card in the casino anymore.

How to Get COMPS

(Overbetting in order to get more comps is a very poor way to gamble.)

Comp is short for complimentary. The *comp*, as it's referred to in casino jargon, is nothing more than a <u>complimentary gift</u> given to a player by the casinos as a reward for gambling. It's there to keep them happy and get them to be returning players. In today's casinos, comps are no longer the privilege of only high rollers. Anybody can get a comp, even if they don't play on a regular basis.

Anybody who risks their money in the casino would be foolish not to go for their comps. Make sure that if you want to get a comp, you ask for it—the floor persons are not going to offer them to you.

There are many different types of comps. A common comp is free parking, if otherwise you would have to pay for it. Or if there is free parking, you can then get free valet parking. Other possibilities include free meals, the cost of shows, free hotel rooms, free golf, tennis (or any other recreational activities). Sometimes even free cash, and so on. Take advantage of all the casino offers in any way that you can. To qualify for better comps, you have to play more frequently or become a high roller.

The comp ratings are not based on whether you win or lose. <u>Comps are based on</u> the amount of time you played at the table and the amount of your average wager. Here is how casinos determine how much your action is worth for them. Assuming you play 1 hour at the $10 table:

- Your average bet is $10

- Playing time is 1 hour
- Average hands dealt per hour: 60
- In an hour, you'll give the casino 60x10=$600 worth of action
- Casino estimated advantage over the majority of players: 2%
- Casinos will comp players between 30 and 50% of the player's expected loss
- $10 (bet)x60 (hands per hour)=$600(worth of action) x2%= $12

This $12 is your theoretical loss. You can get back an average 40% of that, which is $4.80. *That means you can get comped approximately half of your initial bet per hour.*

But you can do even better than this.

If you play a good solid strategy, the house's advantage will be around 0.5%. If you slow down the play (play at a full table, the dealer is slow, or you slow him down, take walks, etc.), you will probably play only 40 hands per hour.

Sticking to my previous example, your theoretical expected loss will be:

$10 x 40 hands x 0.005 (0.5%) = $2 per hour, but you will still get the $4.80 comp per hour. Not too bad.

Above and beyond this calculation, the casinos will also recognize how long (how many years) and how frequently you play in the given casino. The longer you play with them, the more comps you are able to get.

Therefore, as soon as you sit down at the table, present your comp or player's card so that the more you play, the better your rating will be. Identify yourself as a player with a card each time you begin a new session at a new table. You don't have to worry about being recognized. If you play with small bets, it doesn't matter, and if you play with larger bets, then they will know who you are with or without a card. Make sure that all your time spent at the table is recorded.

I am not saying you should go to play only for comps. Betting higher than your bankroll allows, or gambling more often (for a longer period of time) just in order to get more comps is a very poor way to gamble. What I am saying is that if you're playing anyway, you should take whatever is offered for free.

Don't expect them to hand you a comp. They never will give it to you without asking. You have to ask for it again and again. Even if you are not a frequent player at one particular casino, it will quite often happen that your request for a meal will be granted simply because the casino wants to keep you in action.

Here are two examples from my own experience:
A. I was playing for about two hours at a $25 table.

I asked for a dinner voucher, and the pit boss told me, "You are playing on the negative side. Sorry but you cannot have it."

I made a quick calculation. By the casino's determination, I put about $3,000 into action (remember: average 60 hands per hour, 2x60x25=3000). They calculated +/-2% loss over the masses of players. They expected to win ($3000 x 2%) about $60.

Casinos will give players comps worth 30–50% of the expected loss. I was sure it was enough for a buffet voucher.

On top of that, I knew that this casino was taking into consideration how frequently we play and for how many years. In this particular casino, I've been playing for eight years and about 20–25 days per year.

I did not understand his decision. I went to the VIP desk and asked again. In about a second, I received my free dinner voucher! Presumably I just wasn't worthy enough for the pit boss.

I don't want to tell you that they distribute the comps with friendly feelings, but don't be shy to ask for it.

B. It happened in the same casino two weeks later. I went with my wife and we had a couple of guests with us. I wanted to make sure I had enough comps to invite them for dinner in case we wanted to have dinner at the casino.

After lunch I went to the VIP desk and asked, "Do I have enough for dinner for four?"

"Oh, sure," said the gentleman behind the desk.

I didn't take it, because in the meantime my wife mentioned our guests might be interested in going elsewhere for dinner.

I played another two hours then took a walk. My guests had a great time, and we decided we would stay at the casino for dinner. Right before dinner, I went back to pick up my dinner vouchers.

To my surprise, the young woman behind the desk told me, "Sir, you do not have enough for four."

I explained to her that about four hours ago a gentleman told

me I had enough. I also explained that since then, I had played another two hours.

"That's what he said?" she asked.

"Yes," I replied.

"Okay, if he said that, you got it." With this, she presented me with the vouchers for four dinners.

Maybe she was just in such a mood that she wanted to save some money for her employer. This was the moment that I realized although every casino has its own guidelines about how to provide comps, they are very flexible.

Getting the free meals proved that it never hurts to ask.

A Few Good Secrets for the ROOKIES

(To be in the casino only for action is the attitude of losers.)

At one time everybody was a rookie. To be a rookie in itself does not mean anything. There is no advantage and no disadvantage. What bothers me is if a rookie sits down to play without even learning the absolute basics. For example, how to ask for a card, how to signal to stand, what insurance means, etc. If on top of that he has no clue about basic strategy (I'm convinced if somebody doesn't know the basic strategy, then they have even less knowledge about money management, not to mention self-control), then I believe it is a total waste of time to start playing in a bona fide game. This type of player is not a 100% but a 200% sure loser.

If you play blackjack based on instincts, and pay little or no attention to basic strategy and these blackjack secrets, you will be facing a house edge of between 3% and 6%.

Although you can bring the edge to a low level in blackjack, the game is not possible to beat consistently. This is one of the most important of all the blackjack secrets to keep in mind. Nobody can always win. Accept that losses are a part of the game.

You can pick up the absolute basics in any casino, because they teach the game. Don't be too ecstatic with yourself after listening to their thirty-minute presentation. In most cases they introduce nothing but the basic rules of a given game. A half-hour lesson is not enough to jump into an unknown game. Observe, watch how people play the game, but first of all, read as many books as you can. You have to develop your knowledge, winning attitude, and self-control. Without self-control and a winning attitude, nobody can win. By a winning attitude, I mean that you should not play just for the play itself—play to win. The goal of a winning player is to win, and the goal of a beginner is just to play. Don't be there just to get action. To be there for action only is a typical attitude of the losers.

It's never a problem if others know you are a rookie. You will realize if you are a well-prepared rookie you'll know more than a lot of other (not-so-rookie) players. Don't be shy to ask anything, especially the types of things that are hard to pick up from books or that you did not understand. Ask for comps because they do not depend on whether you are a novice or an expert.

Since I believe the quality of other players at the table doesn't have an effect on winning or losing, then consequently (theoretically) it doesn't matter <u>where you sit.</u> Many people believe the decision of the anchor has a substantial effect on the other players. I know it does not. You don't want to give an opportunity to the others to make a comment, however. You don't want to expose yourself to needless comments. If you are a beginner, you should not sit in the third-base spot. Not just because in many casinos the tables are so close to each other (even the $25, $50 tables included) that the first base and the anchor seats are totally uncomfortable, but because that way you can avoid some ignorant players' comments who might blame you for their losses, even if you made the right decisions. But regardless of this, don't play anchor until you are a developing player. I suggest the seat next to the third-base position. If you sit there, you have more time to think about your decisions.

I believe that, if the dealer is helpful and friendly, they make the game more enjoyable for you. <u>Dealers can be helpful</u> for the novice player. For a beginner, sometimes a helpful piece of advice can be most beneficial and profitable. For instance, when the dealer gives a friendly warning to the beginner that he has a doubling down situation. With a small tip, you can make the dealer "your friend." The tip will not change the face of any card, but you may gain a few good tidbits of advice and expand your knowledge. The cards are not going to start performing better just because you tipped the dealer, and remember that it cuts into your winnings. Whatever the reason to tip, there is no question that tipping a dealer doesn't affect the outcome of the game.

It bothers a lot of people to play <u>head-to-head</u> with the dealer. This is perhaps particularly the case for beginners, and it is understandable. In fact, if you are a beginner, I don't recommend it. After a bit of practice, however, this situation can actually be appealing. Going head-to-head is one of my favorite game options because I determine the speed of the game and I don't have to adapt myself to anyone else's play. A lot more hands can be dealt in a given amount of time, but more importantly, going head-to-head gives you a better chance to handle a dealer—you can make him "your friend."

I strongly suggest that you don't play <u>one and two deck</u> games until you have a fair bit of experience. These types of games put more pressure on beginners and are usually not available at tables with lower table minimums.

If you're a beginner, I don't recommend that you play more than one hand at a time.

It comes from the nature of the game that if you play at one table for an extended period of time, players will come and go. If you feel uncomfortable because of any kind of change, don't hesitate to leave the table. Don't become too "addicted" to a particular table. Move. The only exception to this is if you are in the middle of a winning streak. In that case, don't even think about changing tables no matter what the circumstances are. Stay. If somebody leaves the table when they have a winning streak—just because he cannot tolerate somebody or something at the table—it's a sure symptom that they need to practice self-control.

Let me show you a few <u>common mistakes made by rookies</u> so that you can avoid them.

Check the table minimum before you sit down. One of the most humbling feelings when you walk into a crowded casino is when you suddenly find a table with a lot of empty seats. As a rookie, you're happy, you jump in the game, buy in $100, and put out your five-dollar bet. Then the dealer says, "This is a fifty-dollar table, sir!" Every table has the sign with the minimum and maximum bets stated on it.

You have to put your bet <u>into the betting square</u>. It must be in a single stack, in such a form that the higher denominations are at the bottom of the stack.

The dealer must be able to recognize your initial bet if it comes to a double down or split.

You <u>cannot touch your bet</u> after the deal has begun. The reason is because the dealer may think that you are trying to cheat and are attempting to press your bet if you received a good hand. For the same reasons, never put your double down or split bet on the top of your original bet.

In a face-up game, you're <u>not allowed to touch the cards</u> for any reason. If you want to split a hand, don't touch the cards—just put up an additional bet and the dealer will physically split the cards.

One <u>playing mistake</u> made by rookies is caused by <u>mishandling aces</u> when calculating the hand total that contains an ace. As we know, the ace can count as 1 or 11. The easiest way to count the ace is to consider it a "1" and calculate your hand, and then to add a "10" for any ace in the hand.

Keep your chips organized by color so you can avoid misbetting (one green and red is thirty dollars, versus two reds which are only ten dollars).

Don't try to split non-pairs. Also, in a regular game, you cannot double once the third card has been dealt.

How to Play the "Dangerous" ONLINE Casinos

(It's up to you, but I prefer the land-based casinos.)

Why do I call online gambling "dangerous"? First and foremost, because if you are not prepared enough and do not possess enough self-control, then gambling online could cost you much more than a land-based casino. I will talk about these when I discuss the disadvantages of online gambling.

Online casinos started in the mid-90s, which means that the oldest ones have been operating for over fifteen years. They have expanded so rapidly that at the time of writing this book, there are many thousands in existence. A detailed analysis of these could fill many books; therefore, I will avoid doing this and just touch upon some of the main aspects.

Let me share some useful information with you, if you want to play online.

What are the **advantages**?

- It's very easy to download the software, make a deposit, and start playing.
- There is no travel time/cost.
- There are no distractions, such as loud music, drinks, smoking players, etc.
- You can always play head-to-head and more than one hand with the minimum bet.
- It's easy to use charts and keep records of played hands.
- Table minimum and maximum spreads are much bigger than in brick and mortar casinos ($1–$500).
- You can play many more hands in the same amount of time. For example, on average you can play 100–150 hands per hour. With head-to-head play, it's easy to get 150–200 hands per hour, which is about 3 times the rate of a brick and mortar casino.
- The majority of the big online casinos have 24-hour support, which includes telephone, online chatting, e-mail, etc.

- Most online casinos offer a cash sign-up bonus to attract new players. This is real cash credit deposited into your account. The casino hopes you will enjoy their games and become a regular customer. Most of the bonuses match your initial deposit up to a set maximum limit.

What are the **disadvantages**?

- You can turn into an addict very quickly, since the casino is always accessible.
- Albeit a few casinos offer live dealers, the game turns very impersonal. If you are playing alone, it becomes very boring and it's easy to lose control.
- Since after each round used cards are returned to the deck and the deck is shuffled, they are always dealing the first hand (just like in land-based casinos when they use continuous shuffling machines). This is disadvantageous to the player.
- Re-splitting a split hand is usually not permitted.
- The dealer will not always check for blackjack. If the player doubles and the dealer's first card is of value 11 (ace), and the dealer gets blackjack, the player loses both his bets.
- When you buy-in, it usually doesn't take longer than thirty seconds. Cashing out is not always as easy. It takes much longer due to security reasons. You have to provide your address, ID, etc. If you requested a

bank draft, it could take 2–3 weeks to get your money back.

- The cash-in bonus—which seems like an advantage and is generally 100% up to a max of $100—is usually connected to higher betting requirements. For example, it's required that you bet 20–40 times the bonus before you can cash out. An average player will (most of the time) lose the bonus with his initial deposit before meeting the minimum bonus betting requirement. In most of the casinos, this bonus promotion is excluded from the game of blackjack.

- It's almost impossible to know where the casino is located, who or which company owns it, etc.

- It's hard to verify whether the cards are actually dealt in random, as unexpectedly long losing streaks occur.

- It's hard to verify the overall legitimacy of the game.

- They know everything about you. They keep full records on you—they know exactly when and how much you won or lost.

- The biggest disadvantage is that the dealer busts less than expected. The theoretical bust for the dealer is 28.36%. A lot of the online casinos set the software in such a way that the dealer will only bust 19–20% of the time.

In comparing the advantages versus the disadvantages, I feel that the scale tips toward the disadvantages. I recommend online play for practice. It's a chance to try to learn more and to get more experience. But playing for real money? It's up to you. After all, it's your money. I prefer the land-based casinos.

Below, I will give some examples of "good advice" from the Internet. These are so bad that I won't provide which sites the information was derived from simply because I don't want to give them free advertising. Primarily I offer these for entertainment purposes, since you cannot learn much from them other than perhaps to not listen to bad tips.

You can ask how anybody (mostly a rookie) can recognize whether a tip is good or useless. There is no easy answer to this question. When you get more experienced, you will be able to distinguish between them much more easily. The truth is, however, that when you become more experienced, you will not need the advice given by websites. This is the old catch-22.

Check how the given website (online casino) determines the object of the game. If they did not give the correct answer, you can start to doubt everything else. If the site doesn't seem to be well organized, it doesn't inspire confidence. If they try to convince you that everything is very easy and to just jump in, forget them.

The *italics* below are quotes from various websites. My comments follow.

"You are initially dealt a 6 and an ace. This would give you a hand of either 7 or 17. It's your choice. Even if it may not be the wisest move in this case, you could safely draw an additional card."

May not be the wisest move? No, it's not your choice. To hit soft 17 is a must all the time. If somebody doesn't hit soft 17, it's a sign that he is not just a novice but also a sure loser.

"Since a casino can be very noisy, hand signals are usually the preferred method of signaling hit, stand, etc."

I'm afraid this author just doesn't know that hand signals are the preferred method of signaling hit, stand, etc., not because of noise, but first and foremost because of the eye-in-the-sky (cameras).

"As you see, everything in online blackjack is very simple: ace is considered 1 or 11, picture cards are all 10 and all the rest are their face value. The score is calculated by simply summing up the score of all cards that you have at hand."

Yes. Blackjack is very simple. Mainly if we are only talking about how to count our hand's total.

"If you split two aces you are only entitled to one additional draw for each ace. In this case, drawing a ten to an ace is not considered natural and won't cause a tie because it'd be beaten by a blackjack."

Really? Ouch.

So it'd be beaten by a blackjack.

So the dealer didn't check for blackjack before I split? How forgetful.

So I can lose getting a 10 to an ace.

So if it would not be beaten by a blackjack, it will cause a tie? Nice hopes. Or the writer has no idea what he's talking about.

"Insurance - if the dealer turns up an ace he will offer insurance to the players. The choice of insurance allows a player to bet up to half of his original bet against the dealer's blackjack. The dealer will check for blackjack; in case he does the player will lose his original bet but the insurance bet will be paid out at double odds effectively covering the original bet. If the dealer does not have blackjack the player loses both bets."

Oh, what a nice trick to get my money! I hope you understand. If the dealer does not have blackjack, the player loses <u>both</u> bets. I hope you not only understand but know not to play any online casinos where you can lose your original bet if the dealer doesn't have a blackjack.

"Do not assume that the hole card [the dealer's card that's left face down] is of 10 points. Actual mathematical likelihood is under 1/2 so such assumption is pointless."

True. But we are after cases when we are in trouble. The hole card could be 7, 8, 9, or ace and we are still in trouble. This is already 8 of 13 cards or 61.5%.

Looking at it this way, we are already over ½. Be careful with the numbers because you'll find yourself in a similar situation as a "simple" tradesman when asked about how his business is doing. "Not really good, I don't make too much money. I buy something for a hundred bucks and sell for twice as much. This 2% is my profit."

"Never take insurance when offered. Only take insurance if you have a gut feeling that the dealer has blackjack, or if you are card counting and aware of the cards remaining in the deck."

Do you understand? "Never take it" but "only take it"? Playing blackjack by a gut feeling? Lots of players do this exact thing. They are the losers.

I left to the end <u>my all-time "favorite."</u>

"A tie or a push is a game resolution where both win [equal score or natural hands] or bust. When tie occurs, your bet is returned to you."

Here we go! This is exactly what I'm looking for. A game where I can get back my bet when both bust! This is fantastic. Where is this casino? It would be easy to make a few million dollars in a very short period of time. What a dream. Sorry, I was dreaming. Or maybe just the website author.

Miscellaneous (Luck, Myths, Card Counting,
Well-Balanced, Stories)

- 21.1 Don't Believe in Luck in the Long Term
- 21.2 Myths
- 21.3 Card Counting
- 21.4 Time, Patience, and Being Well-Balanced
- 21.5 Stories

21.1 — *DON'T BELIEVE IN LUCK IN THE LONG TERM*
(*To believe in luck is only a bad excuse for players who are too lazy to learn how to play.*)

It's always been a question. How does luck affect the outcome of the game?

Generally if you ask, does luck affect the game? I say, "I don't know."

If you ask, "Does luck affect the game in the short term?" I say, absolutely. In the short term, luck plays a major role in the outcome of the game.

If you ask, "Does luck affect the game in the long term?" I say, not at all, because in the long term, luck will balance out during your lifetime, and the only things that count are your knowledge and, primarily, your self-control.

Luck usually runs in cycles. There will be as many lucky days as unlucky days. If you have a bad day, don't blame your bad luck on the dealer. The dealer is only doing his job. He will not gain anything if he takes your money. Do not give him a hard time. There will always be a few players who do just this. Do not be a partner for those players. Do not ever complain to dealers.

While luck will balance out during a lifetime, your knowledge and self-control won't.

Does knowledge and self-control help players during an *unlucky session*? Yes. How? These skills will help *minimize* your losses (although you must remember that, no matter how good a player you are, you will have some losing sessions). How does knowledge and self-control help players in _lucky sessions_? These elements will _maximize_ your profit.

When we enter the casino, nobody can tell whether or not we will be lucky on that particular day. We have no control over luck, but we have control over the game depending on how good our knowledge and self-control are. This is—much rather than luck—what separates the winners from the losers.

21.2 — MYTHS

(*You can't win a significant amount of money in comparison to your initial bet.*)

There are a lot of **myths** surrounding common knowledge of the game. Some of them have or could have validity, but most myths are just that—myths, without any research conducted to substantiate them. It doesn't matter how they came into existence, it's time to forget them. Let me show you just a few examples.

a. One of the oldest ones is that you need luck in order to win. We've spoken about this (and I hope you remember); luck has no meaning if you think about the long term. In the long term, everything that has to happen will happen according to what we expect.

b. It's impossible to make money in a game when more than two decks are used. This myth definitely reflects a bad card counter, thinking that it's harder to keep track of a six- or eight-deck game because of the number of cards. I don't believe in card counting anymore anyway, but one deck, two decks, eight decks—it doesn't matter. If you're a competent player, then you are just as able to make money with eight decks as you are with two. If you're a recreational player with very limited knowledge, then you will lose regardless of a single-deck or a six-deck game.

c. A bad player at a table hurts the chances of others. It's simply not true. Their decisions help just as often as they hurt. Just like with luck, in the long term, they do not affect others.

d. The decision of the anchor has the biggest impact on the dealer's final hand. This is not true either. If anybody else has already made a wrong move, it doesn't matter what the anchor does. That move already changed the whole shoe (or game).

e. Here is another myth of the game that has been around practically since the game was invented: "never split fours." I think we can forget this one. If we get a pair of fours, our total is 8, which is not a strong hand. Of course, do not split this against a 7 or higher. But if the dealer shows a 4, 5, or 6, he is weak—so why not?

Sure. Split them. If you get another 4, split again! We can argue whether we should split a 4 against a 4 or just hit it. I can tell you that neither of the two possibilities are wrong or right. I always split in these circumstances. First of all, the dealer has a very good chance to bust. On top of that, we have a chance to get a card and double down.

f. Another myth is that you can win a significant amount of money constantly if you follow the advice of any given book. I have to let you know that you can't win a *significant* amount of money in comparison to the money that you employ as your initial bet. As we know, blackjack is a game where the payoff is generally even money. It is just simply unrealistic to expect—for instance—to make a hundred times your initial bet. If you want to do something like this, play roulette for instance, for if you are lucky enough and win a single-number bet, the payoff is 1:35.

g. In order to win a significant amount of money, you need thousands of dollars. It's true and not true. With this, I mean, what do you consider a significant amount of money? I truly believe there is no way

in the long term to achieve more than 2–3 units (of your initial bet) profit per hour. Taking this into consideration, you can calculate what you can expect according to your bankroll.

21.3 — CARD COUNTING

Let me give you my thoughts on **card counting**. Here is what I wrote in my first book (*The Most Powerful Blackjack Manual*): "I believe that card counting is history. In the casino of the post-1990s, there is no need for card counting, which lost its importance the same moment the casinos did the necessary 'counter move' and introduced the use of multiple decks, quick shuffles, and some other rule changes, including table maximums. Consequently, I don't see any good reason under today's casino's circumstances to put any energy into card counting, since we cannot gain any advantage from doing so."

I believe when authors suggest that thousands of people are making a living from blackjack they are just adding to the myth of card counting. Since I have no doubt that in a game dealt from a shoe and the use of a continuous shuffling machine card counting has no meaning, the only chance then remains in a single- or double-deck game. Have you never seen a dealer reshuffle when your big bet is out?

I'm willing to bet—since I personally studied and tried for years to count cards in real casino action—that the majority of authors, giving special consideration to online site authors, present an inadequate knowledge of card counting. This is why it surprises me that some authors, after taking a negative position toward card counting, still "dedicate" a chapter to it, sometimes referring to it as casual card counting. Does it make sense to write about counting if somebody is against it?

Individual card counting doesn't provide enough of an added advantage compared to the effort it requires. The vast majority of people are not even able—not primarily because of their abilities but because of a lack of patience, endurance, etc. It's very tiring work. Don't let yourself be influenced by various authors and websites that suggest it's very easy to learn and to make money. It's not easy. It's tough and primarily you cannot make money doing it. Based on current playing conditions, card counting is just a waste of your time. If you still seriously believe in card counting, here are just some of the questions you should ask yourself:

1. Continuous shuffling machines shuffle after every hand. Therefore, you always get the first hand, where the count is zero.

2. Six-deck games where—thanks to the deep cut—two decks have been cut and we just hope the cards are equally spread.

3. The penetration on single-deck games is about 60%. With four or more players usually a max of two hands are dealt.

Let me tell you about *card counting at online casinos.* It looks like it's easy to count at home, making notes and keeping records. Don't get too excited. In online casinos, card counting does not work at all because the software likes to reshuffle the decks after every hand.

21.4 — *TIME, PATIENCE, AND BEING WELL-BALANCED*

You have to have **time, patience,** and you have to be **well-balanced**.

The game is just like hunting. You are "hunting." Hunting for a good table, hunting for the best circumstances, hunting for a good run, hunting for money. Just like a good hunter. If you do not have the patience to wait for the prey (a good shoe, a good winning streak), then you have no chance at all. The "hunting" that goes on within a casino is not a collaboration. It's solitary. If you are going with friends (i.e., a party of four, six, or eight), you can have a lot of fun, but nothing else. If you're not totally relaxed, ready, and well-balanced, then you cannot play. You cannot gamble in a rush. Leave your negative attitude (if you have one) at home. You can only play with a 100% positive attitude.

A lot of players say they don't care if they lose, they just want to have a **good time**. I'm not saying to go for a bad time. What I am saying is that I'm not going only to have a good time. I'm going to make money. My point is that making money <u>and</u> having a good time are not mutually exclusive.

If we are talking about having a good time, let me tell you this. When you play, do not drink **alcohol.** If you see anybody drinking alcohol at the table, you can be sure he is a recreational player. He is a loser! The casinos know this, which is why they offer free drinks. Sure, you can have a couple of good beers—after you've finished playing!

You cannot be overly **involved emotionally** in the game. If you see somebody who is too happy at getting a blackjack, then you already know that he is a beginner. This game is not for the neurotic, especially not for those who throw a "fit" every time the dealer shows a face card, saying, "A picture, again?!" These players are the sure losers.

Escalating the bet after winning seems like we are playing with the house's money. Many books say to place small bets with your own money and larger bets with the house's money. You cannot forget that **you never play with the house's money**. As soon as you have won it and it's in front of you, it's your money. If someone raises their bets too aggressively, and fails to cash some of the winnings before the loss appears, then one loss can be very frustrating (especially after a bigger split and double).

If you are not a beginner, don't play at a casino's **lowest minimum bet table**. All the beginners, weak players, drinkers . . . all the losers are playing there. Usually the game is very slow. The dealer is teaching them, and they are "teaching" each other. You don't want to belong to that group. You don't need anything that will take away from your focus or that will throw you off balance. At those tables, there are a lot of things to worry about. You can have a lot of fun, you can enjoy yourself, but never will you be able to make decent money in the long term on a constant basis.

21.5 — STORIES

In conclusions, let me entertain you with two of my favorite **stories**:

The biggest dimwit I've seen at the blackjack table.

A heavier-set gentleman sat down to the table, and after a minute, everybody could see he was not an expert.

He gets two aces.

"Can I split them?" he asks the dealer.

"Sure you can," answers the dealer.

He puts an additional green chip on the top of his original bet.

The dealer takes the chip, puts it next to the original one, and explains how to signal if he wants to split and where to put the chip.

After our guy gets a 3 and a 4, he asks for an additional card.

"You can only have one card on an ace," explains the dealer.

"Oh, sorry! I didn't know that."

On the next hand, the guy gets an ace and a 3, while the dealer shows a king.

The guy waves the hand off.

"Sir, this is FOUR or fourteen. It's a free card, you can't go wrong if you ask for another card," says the dealer, trying to help our friend.

"Oh yes, but you told me I can only have ONE card on an ace."

This is not luck. This is skill.

A scrawny man in his early thirties plays the anchor. He keeps talking, laughing, and he is having a great time. However, he has no clue about the game, including of course the basic strategy. He has tremendous luck this day. Every stupid move works for him. He is winning!

His $200 bet is out there. He gets two aces. The dealer shows a 9. He splits them and gets a 3 and a 5. The dealer shows his whole card. It's a deuce. Our man falls silent.

Everybody is stunned.

Then, the dealer takes another deuce. Our fellow starts screaming, "Face, face!!!"

The dealer's next card is a king. He busted.

An older lady turns to our guy, "You are really lucky today!"

Our hero turns very serious.

"No, Mom, this is not luck. This is skill."

A perplexed look falls across the old lady's face.

"I split the aces."